Spencer

N. Eldon Tanner

Marion G. Romney

Ezra Taft Benson

Mark E. Petersen

Marvin J. Ashton

Bruce R. McConkie

L. Tom Perry

Saturday January 14th, 1978   **PRAYER**

Dear Brother and Sister Teerlink...

Thanks for making this special time in our lives even more special.
Best wishes,
Neil and Dear
(Jorgensen)

Spencer W. Kimball

N. Eldon Tanner

Marion G. Romney

Ezra Taft Benson

Mark E. Petersen

Marvin J. Ashton

Bruce R. McConkie

L. Tom Perry

Neal A. Maxwell

Marion D. Hanks

Joseph Anderson

John H. Vandenberg

Robert L. Simpson

S. Dilworth Young

Hartman Rector, Jr.

Carlos E. Asay

Vaughn J. Featherstone

H. Burke Peterson

PRAYER

Deseret Book Company
Salt Lake City, Utah
1977

Library of Congress Cataloging in Publication Data
Main entry under title:

Prayer.

   Includes index.
   1. Prayer—Addresses, essays, lectures. 2. Mormons
and Mormonism—Doctrinal and controversial works—
Mormon authors—Addresses, essays, lectures. I. Kimball,
Spencer W., 1895-
BV210.2.P647   248'.3   77-15521
ISBN 0-87747-657-8

CONTENTS

INTRODUCTION

President N. Eldon Tanner

As a young boy in school, I was greatly impressed by these classic words, which almost every schoolchild has committed to memory:

More things are wrought by prayer
Than this world dreams of. Wherefore, let thy voice
Rise like a fountain for me night and day.
For what are men better than sheep or goats
That nourish a blind life within the brain,
If, knowing God, they lift not hands of prayer
Both for themselves and those who call them friend?
—Alfred, Lord Tennyson
"The Passing of Arthur"

Probably the impression was made because I lived in a home where we prayed individually and as a family, night and morning, every day, and also because I had had my prayers answered at different times and on different occasions. What a wonderful feeling of security it was to know I could call upon the Lord, that he was actually my Father in heaven, that he was interested in me, and that he could hear me and answer my prayers. This knowledge has always been a great source of comfort to me. It has given me confidence and strength when I have needed it most, and the ability to choose and make with confidence decisions that I could not have made otherwise. Having had these experiences, and feeling the need for divine guidance, it has always been my great desire and practice to ask for wisdom and guidance in all of my endeavors.

During my early years I naturally thought that because we prayed in our home, people all over the world had the same belief and were praying to their Heavenly Father. But as I grew older, I learned that many people never pray for guidance, or express their gratitude for the blessings they receive, or return thanks at mealtime for the food they eat. It was still more shocking to learn that there are those who don't even believe

1

in God and therefore do not have faith in him and do not understand that he is a personal God, literally our Father in heaven; that we are his children; and that he can really hear and answer our prayers.

I can never begin to express enough my gratitude to my parents for teaching me this important principle. My father really knew how to talk to the Lord and made him seem so real and near to us. He would pray in the morning, "Let thy blessings attend us as we go about our duties, that we may do what is right and return tonight to report to thee."

I think of that very often, and what a help it is to me! If everyone kept that thought in mind during the day, in all of his activities, knowing that he was going to account to the Lord at night for what he had done that day, it would be a great deterrent to wrongdoing and a great help in accomplishing works of righteousness. It would be my desire that in this book you will find some of the same wonderful spirit and learn some of the same valuable principles that helped my father teach his children to talk to the Lord.

The Lord has admonished parents to teach their children to pray and to walk uprightly before him. This is our most important obligation to our children—to teach them that they are the spirit children of their Heavenly Father, that he is real, that he has great love for his children and wants them to succeed, that they should pray to him to express gratitude and ask for guidance, realizing that faith in him will bring them greater strength, success, and happiness than they can receive from any other source.

We as parents must teach by example and let the efficacy of prayer in our own lives show our children the value of faith in God. How sad to deprive children of the great blessing of learning to know God and learning to depend on him for the comfort and strength and guidance they need so badly in order to cope with the problems of the day. It is equally sad when children are not taught that everything they have comes from God and that they should express their gratitude and strive to be worthy of the blessings they receive.

You remember the story of the ten lepers whom Jesus healed. When one returned to give thanks, the Savior said: "Were there not ten cleansed? but where are the nine? There are not found that returned to give glory to God, save this stranger." (Luke 17:17-18.) The sin of ingratitude is grievous.

As we give thanks for our blessings and pray for our own needs, we should be conscious of others who need our faith and prayers. When we pray for Heavenly Father to bless the poor, the sick, and the needy, and to comfort those who mourn, we must follow our words with our deeds and be actively engaged in serving our fellowmen and ministering to their needs. We are the ones through whom the Lord accomplishes his purposes, and when we are blessed, we should in turn bless others.

We had a sweet experience in our family. As we finished calling upon the Lord in family prayer one evening, one of my daughters said, "Daddy, we have so many blessings, and so much to be thankful for, I wonder if we should ask the Lord for more blessings or if we should thank him for what we have and ask him to help us to be worthy of the blessings we now enjoy." I want to emphasize the importance of making ourselves worthy to accept all that our Father in heaven constantly bestows upon us.

It is easy to pray and give thanks when all is going well and we feel blessed and prosperous. The real test of our gratitude and love for the Lord is in our ability to do as Job did when his trials and tribulations seemed to be almost more than he could endure. He still gave thanks, praised the Lord, and said with all humility and sincerity, "I know that my Redeemer liveth." (See Job 19:25.)

Our Father in heaven knows our needs better than we. He knows what is for our good and the things we need to overcome in order to further our development and progression. We must learn to accept his will in all things, with the faith and assurance that in the end everything he does for us will redound to our good.

It is so important that parents call their children together night and morning, every day, and give each member of the family, one by one, the privilege of addressing the Lord on behalf of the family, expressing gratitude for the many blessings the family has received, and concern for individual and family problems. It is important for each person to ask for guidance in the morning, with the knowledge that he will report at night. Children should learn early in life that they can call upon their Father in heaven.

Each of us should be willing and ready to call on our Father in heaven every day. In this volume, men who have been chosen by our Father in heaven to serve him in this world give counsel to help those who are seeking to know more about prayer. They share with us a message of great importance, the message that this experience called prayer is the most important and vital of all communication.

May we all discover, if we have not already done so, that prayer is a vibrant, vital link with our Father in heaven that gives meaning and purpose to our lives, and that eternal happiness and progress can come only to those whose God is the Lord.

WHY THE LORD ORDAINED PRAYER

Elder Bruce R. McConkie

On the west wall of the Council of the Twelve room in the Salt Lake Temple hangs a picture of the Lord Jesus as he prays in Gethsemane to his Father. In agony beyond compare, suffering both body and spirit, to an extent incomprehensible to man—the coming torture of the cross paling into insignificance—our Lord is here pleading with his Father for strength to work out the infinite and eternal atonement.

Of all the prayers ever uttered, in time or in eternity—by gods, angels, or mortal men—this one stands supreme, above and apart, preeminent over all others.

In this garden called Gethsemane, outside Jerusalem's wall, the greatest member of Adam's race, the One whose every thought and word were perfect, pled with his Father to come off triumphant in the most torturous ordeal ever imposed on man or God.

There, amid the olive trees—in the spirit of pure worship and perfect prayer—Mary's Son struggled under the most crushing burden ever borne by mortal man.

There, in the quiet of the Judean night, while Peter, James, and John slept, God's own Son—with prayer on his lips—took upon himself the sins of all men on conditions of repentance.

Upon his Suffering Servant, the great Elohim, there and then, placed the weight of all the sins of all men of all ages who believe in Christ and seek his face. And the Son, who bore the image of the Father, pled with his divine Progenitor for power to fulfill the chief purpose for which he had come to earth.

This was the hour when all eternity hung in the balance. So great was the sin-created agony—laid on him who knew no sin—that he sweat great drops of blood from every pore, and "would," within himself, that he "might not drink the bitter cup." (D&C 19:18.) From creation's dawn to this supreme hour, and from this atoning night through all the endless ages of eternity, there neither had been nor would be again such a struggle as this.

"The Lord Omnipotent who reigneth, who was, and is from all eternity to all eternity," who had "come down from heaven among the children of men" (Mosiah 3:5); the Creator, Upholder, and Preserver of all things from the beginning, who had made clay his tabernacle; the one person born into the world who had God as his father; the very Son of God himself—in a way beyond mortal comprehension—did then and there work out the infinite and eternal atonement whereby all men are raised in immortality, while those who believe and obey come forth also to an inheritance of eternal life. God the Redeemer ransomed men from the temporal and spiritual death brought upon them by Adam's fall.

And it was at this hour that he, who then bought us with his own blood, offered the most pleading and poignant personal prayer ever to fall from mortal lips. God the Son prayed to God the Father, that the will of the one might be swallowed up in the will of the other, and that he might fulfill the promise made by him when he was chosen to be the Redeemer: "Father, thy will be done, and the glory be thine forever." (Moses 4:2.)

True, as an obedient son whose sole desire was to do the will of the Father who sent him, our Lord prayed always and often during his mortal probation. By natural inheritance, because God was his father, Jesus was endowed with greater powers of intellect and spiritual insight than anyone else has ever possessed. But in spite of his superlative natural powers and endowments—or, shall we not rather say, because of them (for truly the more spiritually perfected and intellectually gifted a person is, the more he recognizes his place in the infinite scheme of things and knows thereby his need for help and guidance from Him who truly is infinite)—and so by virtue of his superlative powers and endowments, Jesus above all men felt the need for constant communion with the Source of all power, all intelligence, and all goodness.

When the time came to choose the twelve special witnesses who should bear record of him and his law unto the ends of the earth, and who should sit with him on twelve thrones judging the whole house of Israel, how did he make the choice? The inspired account says: "He went out into a mountain to pray, and continued all night in prayer to God." Having thus come to know the mind and will of him whose offspring he was, "when it was day, . . . he chose twelve, whom also he named apostles." (Luke 6:12-13.)

When the hour of his arrest and passion were at hand; when there remained one more great truth to be impressed on the Twelve—that if they were to succeed in the assigned work and merit eternal reward with him and his Father they must be one even as he and the Father were one—at this hour of supreme import, he taught the truth involved as part of his great intercessory prayer, fragments of which are preserved for us in John 17.

When he, after his resurrection—note it well: after his resurrection, he was still praying to the Father!—when he, glorified and perfected, sought to give the Nephites the most transcendent spiritual experience they were able to bear, he did it, not in a sermon, but in a prayer. "The things which he prayed cannot be written," the record says, but those who heard bore this testimony:

"The eye hath never seen, neither hath the ear heard, before, so great and marvelous things as we saw and heard Jesus speak unto the Father;

"And no tongue can speak, neither can there be written by any man, neither can the hearts of men conceive so great and marvelous things as we both saw and heard Jesus speak; and no one can conceive of the joy which filled our souls at the time we heard him pray for us unto the Father." (3 Nephi 17:15-17.)

But here in Gethsemane, as a pattern for all suffering, burdened, agonizing men, he poured out his soul to his Father with pleadings never equaled. What petitions he made, what expressions of doctrine he uttered, what words of glory and adoration he then spoke we do not know. Perhaps like his coming prayer among the Nephites the words could not be written, but could be understood only by the power of the Spirit. We do know that on three separate occasions in his prayer he said in substance and thought content: "Oh my Father, if it be possible, let this cup pass from me: nevertheless not as I will, but as thou wilt." (Matthew 26:39.)

Here in Gethsemane, as he said to his Father, "not my

will, but thine, be done," the inspired record says, "There appeared an angel unto him from heaven, strengthening him.

"And being in an agony he prayed more earnestly: and his sweat was as it were great drops of blood falling down to the ground." (Luke 22:42-44.)

Now here is a marvelous thing. Note it well. The Son of God "prayed more earnestly"! He who did all things well, whose every word was right, whose every emphasis was proper; he to whom the Father gave his Spirit without measure; he who was the only perfect being ever to walk the dusty paths of planet earth—the Son of God "prayed more earnestly," teaching us, his brethren, that all prayers, his included, are not alike, and that a greater need calls forth more earnest and faith-filled pleadings before the throne of him to whom the prayers of the saints are a sweet savor.

In this setting, then, seeking to learn and live the law of prayer so that we, like him, can go where he and his Father are, let us summarize what is truly involved in the glorious privilege of approaching the throne of grace. Let us learn how to do so boldly and efficaciously, not in word only but in spirit and in power, so that we may pull down upon ourselves, even as he did upon himself, the very powers of heaven. Perhaps the following ten items will enable us to crystallize our thinking and will guide us in perfecting our own personal prayers.

1. What prayer is

Once we dwelt in our Father's presence, saw his face, and knew his will. We spoke to him, heard his voice, and received counsel and direction from him. Such was our status as spirit children in the pre-earth life. We then walked by sight.

Now we are far removed from the divine presence; we no longer see his face and hear his voice as we then did. We now walk by faith. But we need his counsel and direction as much as or more than we needed it when we mingled with all the seraphic hosts of heaven before the world was. In his infinite wisdom, knowing our needs, a gracious Father has provided prayer as the means of continuing to communicate with him. As I have written elsewhere:

"To pray is to speak with God, either vocally or by forming the thoughts involved in the mind. Prayers may properly include expressions of praise, thanksgiving, and adoration; they are the solemn occasions during which the children of God petition their Eternal Father for those things, both temporal and spiritual, which they feel are needed to sustain them in all the varied tests of this mortal probation. Prayers are occasions of confession—occasions when in humility and contrition, having broken hearts and contrite spirits, the saints confess their sins to Deity and implore him to grant his cleansing forgiveness." (*Mormon Doctrine*, Bookcraft, 2nd ed., p. 581.)

2. Why we pray

Read

There are three basic and fundamental reasons why we pray:

a. *We are commanded to do so.* Prayer is not something of relative insignificance that we may choose to do if the fancy strikes us. Rather, it is an eternal decree of Deity. "Thou shalt repent and call upon God in the name of the Son forevermore," was his word in the first dispensation. "And Adam and Eve, his wife, ceased not to called upon God." (Moses 5:8, 16.) In our day we are instructed: "Ask, and ye shall receive; knock, and it shall be opened unto you." (D&C 4:7.) Home teachers are appointed in the Church to "visit the house of each member and exhort them to pray vocally and in secret." (D&C 20:47.) And speaking by way of commandment to his latter-day people, the Lord says: "He that observeth not his prayers before the Lord in the season thereof, let him be had in remembrance before the judge of my people." (D&C 68:33.)

b. *Temporal and spiritual blessings follow proper prayer.* As all the revelations show, the portals of heaven swing wide open to those who pray in faith; the Lord rains down righteousness upon them; they are preserved in perilous circumstances; the earth yields her fruits to them; and the joys of the gospel dwell in their hearts.

c. *Prayer is essential to salvation.* No accountable person ever has or ever will gain celestial rest unless he learns to communicate with the Master of that realm. And, "how knoweth a man the master whom he has not served, and who is a stranger unto him, and is far from the thoughts and intents of his heart?" (Mosiah 5:13.)

9

3. Pray to the Father

We are commanded to pray to the Father (Elohim) in the name of the Son (Jehovah). The revelations are perfectly clear on this. "Ye must always pray unto the Father in my name," the Lord Jesus said to the Nephites. (3 Nephi 18:19.) And yet there is an amazing mass of false doctrine and false practice in the churches of Christendom and occasionally even among the true saints.

There are those who pray to so-called saints and plead with them to intercede with Christ on their behalf. The official prayer books of the various sects have some prayers addressed to the Father, others to the Son, and others to the Holy Spirit, and it is the exception rather than the rule in some quarters when prayers are offered in the name of Christ. There are those who feel they gain some special relationship with our Lord by addressing petitions directly to him.

It is true that when we pray to the Father, the answer comes from the Son, because "there is . . . one mediator between God and men, the man Christ Jesus." (1 Timothy 2:5.) Joseph Smith, for instance, asked the Father, in the name of the Son, for answers to questions, and the answering voice was not that of the Father but of the Son, because Christ is our advocate, our intercessor, the God (under the Father) who rules and regulates this earth.

And it is true that sometimes in his answers, Christ assumes the prerogative of speaking by divine investiture of authority as though he were the Father; that is, he speaks in the first person and uses the name of the Father because the Father has placed his own name on the Son.

It is also true that we and all the prophets can with propriety shout praises to the Lord Jehovah (Christ). We can properly sing unto his holy name, as in the cry "Hallelujah," which means *praise Jah,* or *praise Jehovah.* But what we must have perfectly clear is that we *always* pray to the Father, not the Son, and we *always* pray in the name of the Son.

4. Ask for temporal and spiritual blessings

We are entitled and expected to pray for all things properly needed, whether temporal or spiritual. We do not have the right of unlimited petition; our requests must be based on righteousness. "Ye ask, and receive not, because ye ask amiss, that ye may consume it upon your lusts." (James 4:3.)

Amulek speaks of crops and herds, of fields and flocks, as well as of mercy and salvation, when he lists those things for which we should pray. (See Alma 34:17-29.) The Lord's Prayer speaks of "our daily bread" (see Matthew 6:11), and James urges us to ask for wisdom (see James 1:5), which in principle means we should seek all of the attributes of godliness. Our revelation says, "Ye are commanded in all things to ask of God." (D&C 46:7.) Nephi says, "Ye must not perform any thing unto the Lord save in the first place ye shall pray unto the Father in the name of Christ, that he will consecrate thy performance unto thee, that thy performance may be for the welfare of thy soul." (2 Nephi 32:9.) And the Lord's promise to all the faithful is: "If thou shalt ask, thou shalt receive revelation upon revelation, knowledge upon knowledge, that thou mayest know the mysteries and peaceable things—that which bringeth joy, that which bringeth life eternal." (D&C 42:61.)

It is clear that we should pray for all that in wisdom and righteousness we should have. Certainly we should seek for a testimony, for revelations, for all of the gifts of the Spirit, including the fulfillment of the promise in Doctrine and Covenants 93:1 of seeing the face of the Lord. But above all our other petitions, we should plead for the companionship of the Holy Ghost in this life and for eternal life in the world to come. When the Nephite Twelve "did pray for that which they most desired," the Book of Mormon account records, "they desired that the Holy Ghost should be given unto them." (3 Nephi 19:9.) The greatest gift a man can receive in this life is the gift of the Holy Ghost, even as the greatest gift he can gain in eternity is eternal life.

5. Pray for others

Our prayers are neither selfish nor self-centered. We seek the spiritual well-being of all men. Some of our prayers are for the benefit and blessing of the Saints alone; others are for the enlightenment and benefit of all our Father's children. "I pray not for the world," Jesus said in his great intercessory prayer, "but for them which thou hast given me." (John 17:9.) But he also commanded: "Love your enemies, bless them that curse you, do good to them that hate you, and pray for them which despitefully use you, and persecute you." (Matthew 5:44.)

And so, just as Christ "is the Saviour of all men, specially of those that believe" (1 Timothy 4:10), so we pray for all men, but especially for ourselves, our families, the saints in general, and those who seek to believe and know the truth. Of especial concern to us are the sick who belong to the household of faith and those who are investigating the restored gospel. "Pray one for another, that ye may be healed," James says, with reference to church members, for "the effectual fervent prayer of a righteous man availeth much." (James 5:16.) And as to those who attend our meetings and who seek to learn the truth, the Lord Jesus says: "Ye shall pray for them unto the Father, in my name," in the hope that they will repent and be baptized. (3 Nephi 18:23. See also verse 30.)

6. When and where to pray

"Pray always." (See 2 Nephi 32:9.) So it is written—meaning: Pray regularly, consistently, day in and day out; and also, live with the spirit of prayer always in your heart, so that your thoughts, words, and acts are always such as will please Him who is Eternal. Amulek speaks of praying "both morning, mid-day, and evening," and says we should pour out our souls to the Lord in our closets, in our secret places, and in the wilderness. (See Alma 34:17-29.) Jesus commanded both personal and family prayer: "Watch and pray always," he said; and also, "Pray in your families unto the Father, always in my name, that your wives and your children may be blessed." (3 Nephi 18:15, 21.)

The practice of the Church in our day is to have family prayer twice daily, plus our daily personal prayers, plus a blessing on our food at mealtimes (except in those public or other circumstances where it would be ostentatious or inappropriate to do so), plus proper prayers in our meetings.

7. How to pray

Always address the Father; give thanks for your blessings; petition him for just and proper needs; and do it in the name of Jesus Christ.

As occasion and circumstances require and permit, confess your sins; counsel with the Lord relative to your personal problems, praise him for his goodness and grace; and utter such expressions of worship and doctrine as will bring you to a state of oneness with him whom you worship.

Two much-overlooked, underworked, and greatly needed guidelines for approved prayer are:

a. *Pray earnestly, sincerely, with real intent, and with all the energy and strength of your soul.* Mere words do not suffice. Vain repetitions are not enough. Literary excellence is of little worth. Indeed, true eloquence is not in excellence of language (although this should be sought for), but in the feeling that accompanies the words, however poorly they are chosen or phrased. Mormon said: "Pray unto the Father with all the energy of heart." (Moroni 7:48.) Also, it is "counted evil unto a man, if he shall pray and not with real intent of heart; yea, and it profiteth him nothing, for God receiveth none such." (Moroni 7:9.)

b. *Pray by the power of the Holy Ghost.* This is the supreme and ultimate achievement in prayer. The promise is: "The Spirit shall be given unto you by the prayer of faith" (D&C 42:14), "and if ye are purified and cleansed from all sin, ye shall ask whatsoever you will in the name of Jesus and it shall be done" (D&C 50:29). Of the coming millennial era, when prayers shall be perfected, the scripture says: "And in that day whatsoever any man shall ask, it shall be given unto him." (D&C 101:27.)

8. Use both agency and prayer

It is not, never has been, and never will be the design and purpose of the Lord—however much we seek him in prayer—to answer all our problems and concerns without struggle and effort on our part. This mortality is a probationary estate. In it we have our agency. We are being tested to see how we will respond in various situations; how we will decide issues; what course we will pursue while we are here walking, not by sight, but by faith. Hence, we are to solve our own problems and then to counsel with the Lord in prayer and receive a spiritual confirmation that our decisions are correct.

As he set forth in his work of translating the Book of Mormon, Joseph Smith did not simply ask the Lord what the characters on the plates meant; rather, he was required to study the matter out in his mind, make a decision of his own, and then ask the Lord if his conclusions were correct. (See D&C 8 and 9.) So it is with us in all that we are called upon to do. Prayer and works go together. If and when we have done all we can, then in consultation with the Lord, through mighty and effectual prayer, we have power to come up with the right conclusions.

9. Follow the formalities of prayer

These (though many) are simple and easy and contribute to the spirit of worship that attends sincere and effectual prayers. Our Father is glorified and exalted; he is an omnipotent being. We are as the dust of the earth in comparison, and yet we are his children with access, through prayer, to his presence. Any act of obeisance that gets us in the proper frame of mind when we pray is all to the good.

We seek the guidance of the Holy Spirit in our prayers. We ponder the solemnities of eternity in our hearts. We approach Deity in the spirit of awe, reverence, and worship. We speak in hushed and solemn tones. We listen for his answer. We are at our best in prayer. We are in the divine presence.

Almost by instinct, therefore, we do such things as bow our heads and close our eyes; fold our arms, or kneel, or fall on our faces. We use the sacred language of prayer (that of the King James Version of the Bible—thee, thou, thine, not you and your). And we say Amen when others pray, thus making their utterances ours, their prayers our prayers.

10. Live as you pray

There is an old saying to this effect: "If you can't pray about a thing, don't do it," which is intended to tie our prayers and acts together. And true it is that our deeds, in large measure, are children of our prayers. Having prayed, we act; our proper petitions have the effect of charting a righteous course of conduct for us. The boy who prays earnestly and devoutly and in faith that he may go on a mission, will then prepare himself for his mission. The young people who pray always, in faith, to marry in the temple, and then act accord-

ingly, are never satisfied with worldly marriage. So inter-
twined are prayer and works that having recited the law of
prayer in detail, Amulek then concludes:

"After ye have done all these things, if ye turn away the
needy, and the naked, and visit not the sick and afflicted, and
impart of your substance, if ye have, to those who stand in
need—I say unto you, if ye do not any of these things, behold,
your prayer is vain, and availeth you nothing, and ye are as
hypocrites who do deny the faith." (Alma 34:28.)

We have now spoken, briefly and in imperfect fashion, of
prayer and some of the great and eternal principles that attend
it. There remains now but one thing more—to testify that
these doctrines are sound and that prayer is a living reality
which leads to eternal life.

Prayer may be gibberish and nonsense to the carnal mind,
but to the saints of God it is the avenue of communication
with the Unseen.

To the unbelieving and rebellious it may seem as an act of
senseless piety born of mental instability, but to those who
have tasted its fruits it becomes an anchor to the soul through
all the storms of life.

Prayer is of God—not the vain repetitions of the heathen,
not the rhetoric of the prayer books, not the insincere lispings
of lustful men, but that prayer which is born of knowledge,
which is nurtured by faith in Christ, which is offered in spirit
and in truth.

Prayer opens the door to peace in this life and eternal life
in the world to come. Prayer is essential to salvation. Unless
and until we make it a living part of us so that we speak to our
Father and have his voice answer, by the power of his Spirit,
we are yet in our sins.

> *Oh, thou by whom we come to God,*
> *The Life, the Truth, the Way!*
> *The path of prayer thyself hast trod;*
> *Lord, teach us how to pray.*
> (Hymns, no. 220)

Of all these things I testify, and pray to the Father in the
name of the Son that all of the Latter-day Saints, as well as all
those in the world who will join with them, may—through
prayer and that righteous living which results therefrom—gain
peace and joy here and an eternal fullness hereafter.

WHY
WE SHOULD
PRAY

President Marion G. Romney

Recently someone asked, Why should we pray? We should pray because prayer is indispensable to the accomplishment of the real purpose of our lives. We are children of God. As such, we have the potentiality to rise to his perfection. The Savior himself inspired us with this aspiration when he said:"I would that ye should be perfect even as I, or your Father who is in heaven is perfect." (3 Nephi 12:48.)

No one shall ever reach such perfection unless he is guided to it by Him who is perfect. And guidance from Him is to be had only through prayer. In our upward climb, this mortal experience through which we are now passing is a necessary step. To obtain perfection, we had to leave our pre-earth home and come to earth. During the transfer, a veil was drawn over our spiritual eyes, and the memory of our pre-earth experiences was suspended. In the Garden of Eden, God endowed us with moral agency and, as it were, left us here on our own between the forces of good and evil to be proved—to see if, walking by faith, we would rise to our high potentiality by doing "all things whatsoever the Lord [our] God shall command [us]." (Abraham 3:25.)

The first instruction the Lord gave Adam and Eve, following their expulsion from Eden, was to pray. (See Moses 5:5.)

During his mortal ministry, Jesus taught "that men ought always to pray." (Luke 18:1.)

To the Nephite multitude he said, "Ye must always pray unto the Father in my name." (3 Nephi 18:19.)

In this last dispensation, two years before the Church was organized, the Lord, in a revelation to the Prophet Joseph Smith, said: "Pray always, that you may come off conqueror; yea, that you may conquer Satan, and that you may escape the hands of the servants of Satan that do uphold his work." (D&C 10:5.)

Later he added: "What I say unto one I say unto all; pray

always lest that wicked one have power in you, and remove you out of your place." (D&C 93:49.)

The experience of the brother of Jared dramatizes the seriousness of disobeying the commandment to pray. From the tower of Babel the Lord led the Jaredite colony to the seashore where they "dwelt in tents . . . for the space of four years.

"And . . . at the end of four years . . . the Lord came again unto the brother of Jared, and stood in a cloud and talked with him. And for the space of three hours did the Lord talk with the brother of Jared, and chastened him because he remembered not to call upon the name of the Lord.

"And the brother of Jared repented of the evil which he had done, and did call upon the name of the Lord for his brethren who were with him. And the Lord said unto him: I will forgive thee and thy brethren of their sins; but thou shalt not sin any more, for ye shall remember that my Spirit will not always strive with man; wherefore, if ye will sin until ye are fully ripe ye shall be cut off from the presence of the Lord." (Ether 2:13-15.)

The sin of which he was guilty was neglecting his prayers.

The foregoing scriptures give adequate reasons why we should pray. There seems to be no limitation as to when, where, and what we should pray about.

". . . in every thing by prayer and supplication with thanksgiving let your requests be made known unto God." (Philippians 4:6.)

"Yea, cry unto him for mercy; for he is mighty to save.

"Cry unto him when ye are in your fields, yea, over all your flocks.

"Cry unto him in your houses, yea, over all your household, both morning, mid-day, and evening.

"Yea, cry unto him against the power of your enemies.

"Yea, cry unto him against the devil, who is an enemy to all righteousness.

"Cry unto him over the crops of your fields, that ye may prosper in them.

"But this is not all; ye must pour out your souls in your closets, and your secret places, and in your wilderness.

"Yea, and when you do not cry unto the Lord, let your hearts be full, drawn out in prayer unto him continually for your welfare, and also for the welfare of those who are around you." (Alma 34:18, 20-24, 26-27.)

"Pray in your families unto the Father, always in my name," said the Savior, "that your wives and your children may be blessed." (3 Nephi 18:21.)

"Pray vocally as well as in thy heart; yea, before the world as well as in secret, in public as well as in private." (D&C 19:28.)

"Call upon the Lord, that his kingdom may go forth upon the earth, that the inhabitants thereof may receive it, and be prepared for the days to come, in the which the Son of Man shall come down in heaven, clothed in the brightness of his glory, to meet the kingdom of God which is set up on the earth.

"Wherefore, may the kingdom of God go forth, that the kingdom of heaven may come, that thou, O God, mayest be glorified in heaven so on earth, that thine enemies may be subdued; for thine is the honor, power and glory, forever and ever. Amen." (D&C 65:5-6.)

Prayer is the key that unlocks the door to communion with Deity. "Behold," said the Lord, "I stand at the door, and knock: if any man hear my voice, and open the door, I will come in to him, and will sup with him, and he with me." (Revelation 3:20.)

A similar promise, as Jesus gave it to the Nephites, is: "Whatsoever ye shall ask the Father in my name, *which is right,* believing that ye shall receive, behold it shall be given unto you." (3 Nephi 18:20. Italics added.)

To us of this last dispensation, the promise is thus stated: "Whatsoever ye ask the Father in my name it shall be given unto you, *that is expedient for you.*" (D&C 88:64. Italics added.)

The sacred records are replete with proof that such promises are fulfilled.

Prayer brought forgiveness of sins to Enos. (See Enos 4-5.) The prayers of Alma senior sent an angel to bring his son Alma to repentance. (See Mosiah 27:14.) Prayer brought the Father and the Son to visit the Prophet Joseph Smith. (See Joseph Smith 22:14-17.) Prayer brought the sea gulls from the lake to help save the crops of the pioneers.

Not every prayer brings a spectacular response, but every sincere and earnest prayer is heard and responded to by the

Spirit of the Lord. The manner in which answers to prayer most frequently come was indicated by the Lord when he said to Oliver Cowdery:

"Verily, verily, I say unto you, if you desire a further witness, cast your mind upon the night that you cried unto me in your heart, that you might know concerning the truth of these things.

"Did I not speak peace to your mind concerning the matter? What greater witness can you have than from God?" (D&C 6:22-23.)

To all of us in this last dispensation, the Lord has given this promise: "If you will ask of me you shall receive; if you will knock it shall be opened unto you." In seven different revelations, the Lord repeats this promise verbatim—D&C 6:5, 11:5, 12:5, 14:5, 49:26, 66:9, 75:27.

In the Doctrine and Covenants he further says:

"I say unto you, my friends, I leave these sayings with you to ponder in your hearts, with this commandment which I give unto you, that ye shall call upon me while I am near—

"Draw near unto me and I will draw near unto you; seek me diligently and ye shall find me; ask, and ye shall receive; knock, and it shall be opened unto you.

"Whatsoever ye ask the Father in my name it shall be given unto you, that is expedient for you." (D&C 88:62-64.)

To the truth of these promises, I bear my own testimony; I know they are true.

I know that prayers are answered. Like Nephi and Enos of old, I was born of "just" and "goodly" parents. Early in my childhood I was trained to kneel at my bedside morning and evening each day and thank my Heavenly Father for his blessings and petition him for his continued guidance and protection. This procedure has remained with me through the years.

In answer to prayer as a child, I found my lost toys; as a youth, in answer to prayer, I was led to find the cows in a thicket. I am familiar with the feeling spoken of by the Lord when, to Oliver Cowdery, he said: "Did I not speak peace to your mind concerning the matter?" (D&C 6:23.) He further said: "Behold, I say unto you, that you must study it out in your mind; then you must ask me if it be right, and if it is right I will cause that your bosom shall burn within you; therefore, you shall feel that it is right. But if it be not right you shall have no such feelings, but you shall have a stupor of thought." (D&C 9:8-9.)

I know what Enos meant when he said that "the voice of the Lord came into my mind again." (Enos 10.) By this means I have received in sentences answers to my prayers.

I have witnessed the fulfillment of the Lord's promise that "whoso shall ask . . . in my name in faith, they shall cast out devils; they shall heal the sick; they shall cause the blind to receive their sight, and the deaf to hear, and the dumb to speak, and the lame to walk." (D&C 35:9.)

I have put Moroni's promise to the test and in answer to my prayers I have received a divine witness that the Book of Mormon is true. I further know that by praying "with a sincere heart, with real intent, having faith in Christ," one may "by the power of the Holy Ghost" receive a knowledge of "the truth of all things." (See Moroni 10:4-5.)

I bear my personal solemn testimony that prayer is the key that unlocks the door to communion with Deity.

PREPARATION
FOR PRAYER

Elder Marion D. Hanks

Under Divine Law the blessings of prayer, like salvation, are enjoyed by each individual in that measure which we are "willing to receive," rather than in any inscrutable outpouring or withholding from the heavens. Our loving Father in heaven desires our eternal joy, knows that such joy accompanies true Christ-like character which can only be developed through the proper exercise of our free agency, and so has made available to us the rules for eternal happiness, with his Spirit to guide us; provided a circumstance in which there is "opposition in all things"; and "given unto man that he should act for himself."

Under these principles, we limit what God can do for us by our willful ignorance or disobedience or selfishness or lack of faith. Speaking of those who will not qualify for any of the kingdoms of his glory but accept instead a "kingdom not of glory," he has said through a prophet:

". . . they shall return again to their own place, to enjoy that which they are willing to receive, because they were not willing to enjoy that which they might have received.

"For what doth it profit a man if a gift is bestowed upon him, and he receive not the gift? Behold, he rejoices not in that which is given unto him, neither rejoices in him who is the giver of the gift." (D&C 88:32-33.)

This principle applies also to prayer. We will enjoy the blessings we are willing to receive.

The scriptures repeatedly admonish and invite us to pray, but some of us have never accepted the invitation. Others make occasional attempts at prayer but feel unrewarded, the petition seemingly unheeded. For many, prayer may be largely formula or habit. Perhaps the kind of prayer most widely, if infrequently, experienced has been the pleas of anguish, imploring heavenly intervention in present or pending calamity, or in the aborting of the consequences of some foolish act or unwise decision.

But there are also those who have a rich prayer experience, a prayer life, a consistent, rewarding relationship with the Lord in a real and responsive way. How is that blessing brought about? How can we develop that kind of prayer relationship?

Consider these different experiences with prayer and the results of each, and where we individually may be in the program.

1. It is certain that if we do not pray, we do not receive the blessings of prayer. Like one who has never really enjoyed a great poem or a good book, a painting or a symphony or a sunset, we may live on unaware, missing, perhaps even disdaining, what we will not enjoy. Instead, we experience that which we are willing to receive.

2. Deep need or personal crises motivate some of the most earnest prayers we ever offer. Sin, fear, anxiety, an unsupportable burden—these drive us, rather than beckon us, to prayer. When we are pressed by great affliction or threatened in our personal life, when tribulation is upon us, we turn to God. All who are acquainted with prayer and who have lived long enough to experience life's complexities and vicissitudes understand this kind of reaching for the Lord. We know what it is to cry out to God in sorrowing penitence or deep necessity, or perhaps in great gratitude. The spontaneity of these outcryings—these "groanings" of the soul—is normal and natural and issues from a relationship with our Heavenly Father that is intuitively felt, whether or not nurtured or ever acknowledged to self in comfortable seasons. Such occasions are usually not premeditated or prethought or prepared; they issue from our depths, from anguish or despair or shame or humble gratitude, often with tears, and they signify the reality of that which in every human is more than human, something that identifies us with a power and spirit far loftier and lovelier than our own, with a caring Father with whom we have part as his beloved children.

But such special times of anxiety or fear or exultation of spirit, sincere and important as they are, are like occasional calls home when our more thoughtful and regular attendance would be welcome, and is expected.

3. Less availing, perhaps, are the sporadic efforts that occur when we think we are too tired or too busy, but are

nudged into motion by the remembrance of other times and other circumstances when our faith was more simple or our needs more pressing, and we were not too tired or too busy to pray more consistently and confidently. We pray because we know we ought to pray, and we are responsive enough to take a minute to go through the motions.

4. But suppose we *are* reporting with regularity, but do it merely as a matter of habit, our thoughts elsewhere, our minds inattentive to the communication, our hearts not in it, our words the language learned long ago from others and never changed or challenged through personal needs or matured spiritual strength. Some of us pray like that. We say our prayers by rote, as ritual, missing much of the meaning and purpose of prayer and therefore its value. Not really believing, perhaps not really even paying attention, we may be repeating little phrases from childhood signifying nothing, words without worship, form without feeling, prayer that scarcely leaves our lips, involving neither emotions nor mind nor spirit.

We can and should do better. We can open channels of consolation and courage, and consolidate the powers in our own personality. We can set in motion and put into focus forces we have only heard about or dimly dreamed of and never had faith enough to seek for or really believe in or expect to have functioning in our own behalf.

Twice in recent years accounts have appeared in newspapers of communities suffering from insufficient water supplies and pressure, who have undertaken costly studies and planned extensive improvements only to discover by chance that the main valve of the water system in the towns was only partially open. They had been surviving on a thin stream and weak force when they could have at any time enjoyed vastly enhanced power simply by turning on the valve.

Prayer is like that.

Deep wellsprings of living water are available and accessible to us, a limitless source of spiritual sustenance, of guidance and comfort and divine love.

We can open up the line. That is what preparation for prayer can help us accomplish.

We are not talking about making prayer more difficult, or necessarily longer, or surrounding it with formalities, or making it seem mysterious. Prayer is the simple act of communicating with God; it is an act of worship and usually involves talking and listening. The unspoken "yearnings of our hearts" or the "groanings of the spirit" also go up to God, it is sure. We should pray when we feel like praying, and we should also pray when we do not much feel like praying, and the formalities are obviously of little concern to him. The important thing is to reach out for him in faith and love. But our prayers can mean much more to us and be more effective in bringing about God's purposes for us if we are prepared for the experience in the way he has directed.

The ancient prophet Samuel, speaking to all the house of Israel, said: ". . . prepare your hearts unto the Lord, and serve him only. . . ." (1 Samuel 7:3.)

God's stalwart servant Job, suffering the agonies of his deprivation and pain, was told, ". . . prepare thine heart, and stretch out thine hands toward him." (Job 11:13.)

We are taught that God, who knows our hearts and our needs before we ever come to him, will help us prepare ourselves and in effect speak through us as we pray to him. "The preparations of the heart in man, and the answer of the tongue, is from the Lord." (Proverbs 16:1.)

If the question should be asked, What sense is there in prayer if God already knows our needs and in effect is speaking through us to himself, then the answer is the same answer that applies to all that he expects of us: He wants us to be involved, to have the experience, to make the effort, knowing that only in this way do we really understand, commit our hearts, and grow.

There are many classic cases of preparation preceding prayer. Consider several of these.

1. *Enos.* In his youth Enos had been taught in "the nurture and admonition of the Lord," and the teachings of his father had "sunk deep" into his heart. As he was hunting in the forest one day, the thoughts he had often heard his father speak "concerning eternal life, and the joy of the saints" came to him with such force that his "soul hungered"; and he "kneeled down before [his] maker and . . . cried unto him in mighty prayer and supplication for [his] own soul."

Instruction faithfully and patiently given, quiet contemplation, and that great moment of need when his "soul hungered" combined to bring about a condition in which Enos's prayers to God engendered the most meaningful experience of his life. The marvelous consequences are taught in one short, very significant chapter as the book of Enos in the Book of Mormon.

2. *Nephi.* The record teaches us that Nephi, being very young and "having great desires to know of the mysteries of God, . . . did cry unto the Lord; and behold he did visit me, and did soften my heart that I did believe all the words which had been spoken by my father. . . ." (1 Nephi 2:16.) A boy, patiently and lovingly taught by a good father, early enjoyed the great desire to know for himself, and in the intensity of that desire went to the Lord and received his answer.

3. *Oliver Cowdery.* Oliver Cowdery was promised a knowledge of the Book of Mormon records if he would "ask in faith, with an honest heart, believing." The promise was unequivocal. He would know in his mind and heart by the Holy Ghost, through the spirit of revelation. He was invited to ask that he might know the mysteries of God and that he might "translate and receive knowledge from all those ancient records which have been hid up, that are sacred," with the promise that "according to your faith shall it be done unto you." (D&C 8.)

Oliver tried to translate but did not succeed, and he was told that he had "not understood" but had supposed God would give it to him "when you took no thought save it was to ask me.

"But, behold, I say unto you, that you must study it out in your mind; *then* you must ask me if it be right, and if it is right I will cause that your bosom shall burn within you; therefore, you shall feel that it is right.

"But if it be not right, you shall have no such feelings, but you shall have a stupor of thought that shall cause you to forget the thing which is wrong. . . ." (D&C 9:7-9. Italics added.)

4. *Moroni.* Moroni exhorted the Lamanites that when they should receive the translated record of the Book of Mormon and should "read these things," they should remember the Lord's mercy unto his children from the creation of Adam to the present, and "ponder it" in their hearts. Thus having received, read, meditated, and been grateful, and pondered these things in their hearts, then they were to "ask God, the

Eternal Father, in the name of Christ, if these things are not true." If they should ask "with a sincere heart, with real intent, having faith in Christ," God would manifest the truth unto them by the power of the Holy Ghost. (Moroni 10:3-5.)

In all these accounts there is one consistent message: Preparation for prayer can help communication with the Lord become an experience full of meaning and full of love, and can help to bring about the realization of God's purposes, and of our appropriate purposes, in prayer.

Our *hearts* must be prepared for prayer, for the instruction is that we are to go to him with "all our hearts," with lowliness of heart, with sincerity of heart, with honest hearts, and with broken and contrite hearts.

If our hearts are really right and committed to the Lord, we will go to him with confidence, with, as the psalmist said, "expectations in the Lord," believing that we shall receive. The fullness of our blessings and the soul-satisfying answers to our prayers will come when we learn to "yield our hearts" unto the Lord.

"Nevertheless they did fast and pray oft, and did wax stronger and stronger in their humility, and firmer and firmer in the faith of Christ, unto the filling their souls with joy and consolation, yea, even to the purifying and the sanctification of their hearts, which sanctification cometh because of their yielding their hearts unto God." (Helaman 3:35.)

God expects us to come to him with our spirits in tune, ready to yield our hearts unto him. If we will do this, we have his promise, and we will receive the blessings.

Our *minds* also need to be prepared for prayer. Through search and study we can begin to learn what we need to know. And we must think—actively, consciously, quietly, reflectively, honestly, deeply think. Then we can in good conscience come to the Lord to seek wisdom, comfort, strength, grace, or courage. When we know our own needs, know what we have to be thankful for, know what our responsibility is to God and others, then, with our souls hungry and our desires strong and honest, we can approach the Lord with earnest questions, appropriate petitions, and grateful minds.

As our minds and hearts are prepared, so must our *spirits* be subdued and sensitive if we desire to drink deeply from the spring. We are to go to him in confidence, believing that we shall receive. John assures us: "And this is the confidence that we have in him, that, if we ask any thing according to his will, he heareth us: And if we know that he hear us, whatsover we ask, we know that we have the petitions that we desired of him." (1 John 5:14-15.)

There is another form of preparation for prayer that must be considered, and that is the *condition of our lives* as a testimony of our determination and effort to obey his commandments. One of the most beautiful promises given by the Lord to Joseph Smith was that "if ye are purified and cleansed from all sin, ye shall ask whatsoever you will in the name of Jesus and it shall be done." (D&C 50:29.)

Consistently the scriptures teach that the Lord expects us to approach him with clean hands, having prepared ourselves for the visit. We are to repent and forsake sins, turn away from evil, learn to keep his commandments and to abide in him as his word abides in us.

Our relationship with others must be right. Before we take our gift to the altar, we are to correct matters that separate us from our neighbors. The admonition is to forgive others and to confess our faults and pray for one another as we ask for forgiveness for ourselves. King Benjamin taught his people that they were to believe in God and in his almighty power, to recognize their own limitations, to repent of their sins and forsake them, and to humble themselves before God and ask in sincerity of heart for his forgiveness. (Mosiah 4:9-10.)

The records are clear and understandable. We are to be prayerful and thankful in our hearts always, to seek his presence regularly, and to talk over with him all the matters that concern us, large and small. We are to go to him in times of penitence and in times of gratitude; when we need wisdom, when our souls hunger, when we have need to commune with him. Yet he expects us to come with our minds and hearts right and our spirits in tune, ready to yield our hearts unto him.

In our personal lives, then, and in our homes and families, how shall we prepare for prayer? In all the ways mentioned, with these specific suggestions:

Read the scriptures. When Nephi wrote the story of his father's experience with the Lord, he talked of Lehi's vision in which a person descended out of the midst of heaven and gave Lehi a book and "bade him that he would read. And . . . as he read he was filled with the Spirit of the Lord." (1 Nephi 1:11-12.)

So may we, as we read the scriptures, receive the Spirit of the Lord. The stories from scripture mentioned above, and countless others, will help us get the spirit of prayer. The sacred records speak knowledge and understanding to us, lead to testimony, and offer ways of application to us individually; they will help us to want to pray and lead us to experience prayer.

Fast. This is a wonderful way to prepare ourselves for prayer. Fasting and prayer go together. The subduing of the spirit by the discipline of the appetites is a divinely directed avenue to accomplishing the purposes of prayer.

Meditate. We need to actively, consciously think about the Lord and our relationship with him, about his goodness to us and our forebears, about the gratitude we should feel for all he has given and does now give us. To quietly consider and reflect upon our blessings is an exercise of high value and great benefit.

Discuss these matters with our families before family prayer. We should be calling to the attention of our children and their children the special kindnesses and graciousness of the Lord to us in his gifts, especially the gift of his Holy Son and all that he means to us.

It will bless all of us to think about and speak of our covenants made solemnly in sacred places and renewed regularly through partaking the sacrament. We can share feelings and impressions and experiences with those nearest and dearest to us. This done before prayer will bring tender and humbling sentiments and spiritual emotions to our hearts.

A quiet moment of conversation about our experiences with ourselves, with our families, with others, and with the Lord can be fruitful. What were the good things we did today? What were the actions and language and relationships that were not good? What was the genealogy of our behavior, good or bad, today? What were its roots and how can they be traced to earlier thoughts or behavior? to attitudes we perhaps need to examine? How can we improve?

There are other ways of preparation for prayer. Contemplation of beauty of God's wonderful world, communing with nature in lovely places, experiencing the uplift of great music or great literature, these and other ways bring us enhanced capacity and encourage us, strengthen us, and help us in an attitude of thankfulness and prayerfulness.

In the three essential relationships of life—with ourselves, with others, and with God—there must be unity and wholeness if we are to be happy. Whenever we, through inspiration and determination, through penitence and reconciliation, bring about greater integrity in any of these relationships, we can appropriately approach the Lord seeking his sanctifying Spirit to give divine stamp of approval to our honest efforts. We may come to him in prayer with the certainty that we are heard and that he will help. In our burdens and anxiety and times of moral weakness we have of ourselves no strength sufficient for the need. Why not try God? He is our ready source of power. He wants to help us, and he will help us, according to his great wisdom and his great love and his knowledge of our needs. Of this I personally know, as I know that preparation for praying makes prayer a sweeter and lovelier and more meaningful experience.

May each of us be transformed by the renewing of our minds, and know that which is "good, and acceptable, and perfect" in the Lord.

THE LANGUAGE AND PATTERN OF PRAYER

Elder Carlos E. Asay

Recently two grandsons knelt at my side to join in family prayer. At my invitation, both boys fell to their knees, folded their arms, bowed their heads, and closed their eyes. As I spoke the prayer in behalf of the family, the oldest boy, age two, began to mimic my words. Soon the younger boy, only one year old, was doing the same thing. The sounds made by my grandsons were little more than the babbling of babes; nonetheless, their awkward and sincere attempt to pray, along with their special language of prayer, was very choice, and it touched the hearts of all present.

This experience with Seth and Ben caused me to reflect upon another touching scene—one recorded in the Book of Mormon. In this instance the Savior had instructed the Nephite multitude and healed their sick. Then he taught and administered to the children. It is written: ". . . and he did loose their tongues, and they did speak unto their fathers great and marvelous things, even greater than he had revealed unto the people; . . . yea, even babes did open their mouths and utter marvelous things." (3 Nephi 26:14, 16.)

Reflecting upon the family prayer incident with my grandsons, I am reminded of three things: (1) the inherent desire of all persons, particularly the very young, to commune with the God who gave them life; (2) the need for childlike faith and childlike purity in the conduct of true and acceptable worship, and (3) the responsibility I have to teach my children and grandchildren "to pray, and to walk uprightly before the Lord." (D&C 68:28.)

I don't suspect that I have many responsibilities more important than that of encouraging Seth, Ben, and others to pray in a way that is acceptable to Heavenly Father. If I ever hope to measure up in terms of my parental duties, I must do what is necessary to establish dialogue with God and help loved ones do the same. For unless we, and ours, bridge heaven and earth through prayer, our lives will have little meaning and little direction.

I perceive deep significance in the words of the Savior mentioned above: "And he did loose their tongues, and they did speak unto their fathers great and marvelous things." (3 Nephi 26:14.) How do we loose tongues? How do we open the mouths of babes and the mouths of men and enable them to utter marvelous things? The answers to these questions are apparent—by teaching truth, building faith, and teaching people how to pray.

You will recall that on one occasion the Lord's disciples said to him, "Lord, teach us to pray." (Luke 11:1.) (They might have said: "Loose our tongues and teach us how to speak with our Heavenly Father.") The Savior responded by saying, "After this manner therefore pray ye." (Matthew 6:9.) He then gave to them what is known as the Lord's Prayer. (See Matthew 6:9-13 and Luke 11:2-4.) On another occasion, he taught the Nephites the pattern of prayer. (See 3 Nephi 13:9-13.)

The scriptures contain several accounts wherein the Master and his disciples provided inspired instructions concerning prayer. It is to these selected scriptures that we now turn to obtain insight about the approved form and accepted language of prayer.

Standards of divine excellence

Before outlining and discussing the standards or guidelines of prayer, we should note some introductory instructions. These instructions might well serve as a preface and channel our thinking as the pattern of prayer is presented.

The Lord said: ". . . I will give unto you a pattern in all things, that ye may not be deceived; for Satan is abroad in the land, and he goeth forth deceiving the nations." (D&C 52:14.) He also said: "I give unto you these sayings that you may understand and know how to worship and know what you worship, that you may come unto the Father in my name, and in due time receive of his fulness." (D&C 93:19.) Unless we know God and are acquainted with his ways, how can we "worship him in spirit and in truth"? (John 4:24.) How can we gain salvation through our worship unless we know the true and living God and are prepared to turn to him in true prayer?

True prayer, the type of prayer that exalts the soul and parts the heavens, is based upon faith in God, the Eternal Father, and in his Son, Jesus Christ. In addition to that faith, we must also know how to approach him and how to converse with him in an approved way. Elder Bruce R. McConkie counsels: "Prayers of the saints are expected to conform to a prescribed standard of divine excellence; they should fit into the approved pattern of proper prayer." (Bruce R. McConkie, *Mormon Doctrine*, Bookcraft, second ed., p. 581.)

Salutation

Speaking to his disciples, Jesus said: "After this manner therefore pray ye: Our Father which art in heaven, Hallowed be thy name." (Matthew 6:9.) In one short sentence—a simple yet majestic salutation—the disciples were taught how to begin their prayers and to whom they should direct their words. They were not instructed to address some mysterious or unknown deity. They were told to speak with their Father in heaven, the Father of all spirits. President Marion G. Romney provides this commentary:

"There is a world of difference in the attitude in which one prays understandingly to 'our Father which art in heaven' and that of one whose prayer is addressed to some unknown god thought of as 'cosmic energy,' 'universal consciousness,' or as 'the first great cause.' No man prays to a theoretical god with the faith and expectation that his petition will receive sympathetic personal consideration. But one can understandingly pray to the true and living God with the assurance that his prayers will be heard and answered. When God is believed in as our Eternal Father, we can to a degree understand our relationship to him—that he is the Father of our spirits, a loving parent who is interested in his children individually and whom they can love with all their hearts, might, mind, and strength." (*Look to God and Live*, Deseret Book Co., 1973, p. 201.)

I have always been intrigued by the account of the misdirected (almost satanic) worship of the Zoramites. They not only denounced Christ in their prayers, but they also addressed a false God in a pompous manner. Note the language of their set prayer: "Holy, holy God; we believe that thou art God, and we believe that thou art holy, and thou wast a spirit, and that thou art a spirit, and that thou wilt be a spirit forever." (Alma 31:15.)

Little wonder that Alma and his brethren were astonished and grieved by such worship. These Nephite missionaries must have felt much like Paul when he observed the superstitious worship by the men of Athens as they paid devotion "TO THE UNKNOWN GOD." Paul did not hesitate to correct the Athenians nor did he mince words in issuing this warning: "And the times of this ignorance God winked at; but now commandeth all men every where to repent." (Acts 17:22-30.)

We are taught and we should teach men everywhere to address prayers to our Father in heaven. We should avoid adding flowered and unnecessary descriptions to our salutations. What words can add dignity or honor to the sacred expression, "Our Father which art in heaven"?

Two cautions: As we pray to our Father in heaven, we should avoid using the term "Lord." This is confusing and makes it difficult for us to tell whether we are addressing the Father or his Son, Jesus Christ. Second, we should avoid the unnecessary repetition of the name of Deity. The repeated use of such phrases as "Our Father," "Dear Father," "Holy Father" can detract and become vain repetition. Dr. Royal L. Garff made this succinct statement: "Needless reiterations change the sacred connotations of prayers into redundant utterances."

Expressions of thanks

During the Savior's second visit to the Nephites, he departed out of their midst, bowed himself to the earth, and said: "Father , I thank thee that . . ." (3 Nephi 19:20.) A short time later, he prayed again. He addressed the Father and said: "I thank thee that . . ." (3 Nephi 19:28.) Herein is a significant part of the approved pattern of prayer. It is to acknowledge God's goodnesses and to extend thanks for blessings received.

Ingratitude, we are told, is a sin. If we fail to recognize benefits received from a loving and generous parent, we are indeed ungrateful children. What father is not offended by an unthankful son or daughter who finds it easy to receive and inconvenient to say "thanks"? We do demonstrate our gratitude in the way we act or serve; nonetheless, words of gratitude should be included in our songs of praise and prayers of thanksgiving.

The psalmist sang: "Enter into his gates with thanksgiving, and into his courts with praise: be thankful unto him, and bless his name." (Psalm 100:4.) "O how you ought to thank your heavenly King!" spoke King Benjamin. He added: "I say unto you, my brethren, that if you should *render all the thanks and praise which your whole soul has power to possess,* to that God who has created you, and has kept and preserved you, and has caused that ye should rejoice, and has granted that ye should live in peace one with another— . . . yet ye would be unprofitable servants." (Mosiah 2:19-21. Italics added.)

Petitions

Referring once more to Jesus' prayers among the Nephites, we identify another essential part of the pattern of prayer. It has already been mentioned that he addressed the Father and offered thanks for blessings received. He next used expressions such as: "Father, I pray thee that thou wilt give," "I pray unto thee for them," and "I pray not for the world, but for those whom thou hast given me out of the world." (3 Nephi 19:21, 23, 29.) These words teach us that prayers may properly include requests in behalf of others and petitions for divine assistance, forgiveness of sins, direction, and intervention.

It is not uncommon to hear the Saints pray for the prophet, the General Authorities, and their local priesthood leaders. Petitions to God requesting that the health of Church leaders be preserved, that their lives be extended, and that they continue to enjoy the companionship of the Holy Spirit are certainly timely and appropriate. All such petitions, however, should be prompted by sincere feelings and should not be spoken simply because others have used the same petitions.

Quite often we hear people pray for the full-time missionaries. This too is proper and acceptable, providing our prayers are honest. President Spencer W. Kimball has urged us to pray that the doors of nations will be opened to missionary work. He has pled with us to do all within our power to unlock these doors, but he realizes that divine intervention is requisite in some cases. Once Enos had obtained a forgiveness of his sins, he felt a desire for the welfare of his brethren, the Nephites. He, therefore, poured out his whole soul unto God *for them.* (See Enos 5-9.)

When we speak of petitioning Deity, we instinctively think of Amulek's classic testimony, which included thoughts about prayer. He urged the people to—

"Cry unto him for mercy. . . .

"Cry unto him when ye are in your fields, yea over all your flocks.

"Cry unto him in your houses, yea, over all your household. . . .

"Yea, cry unto him against the power of your enemies.

"Yea, cry unto him against the devil. . . .

"Cry unto him over the crops of your field, that ye may prosper in them.

"Yea, and when you do not cry unto the Lord, let your hearts be full, drawn out in prayer unto him continually for your welfare, and also the welfare of those who are around you." (Alma 34:18, 20-24, 27.)

I have always been impressed by the following counsel: ". . . call on his holy name, and watch and pray continually, that ye may not be tempted above that which ye can bear, and thus be led by the Holy Spirit. . . ." (Alma 13:28.) Such thoughts, such humble expressions are certainly appropriate as we petition God. The Savior's words were: "And lead us not into temptation, but deliver us from evil." (3 Nephi 13:12.)

We have been promised that our Heavenly Father will forgive us of our trespasses if we forgive those who trespass against us. So, it is altogether fitting that we heed the Master's model and pray: "And forgive us our debts, as we forgive our debtors." (3 Nephi 13:11.)

Two related cautions should be mentioned at this point. First, we must be willing to subject our petitions to the will of our Father in heaven. You will recall the Lord's prayer in Gethsemane. Amid pain, agony, blood-sweat, and tears he prayed, ". . . not my will, but thine, be done." (Luke 22:42.) In this instance he was applying that which he had taught his disciples earlier, for he had instructed them to pray, "Thy will be done on earth as it is in heaven." (3 Nephi 13:10.) Anytime we use the language "Thy will be done" or "If it be thy will," it should ring with conviction and never be lip service only. Second, we must atune ourselves to the Spirit so that our petitions are in complete harmony with divine will. Kindly note the following scriptures and the italicized words:

". . . whatsoever ye shall ask in prayer, *believing,* ye shall receive." (Matthew 21:22. Italics added.)

". . . Whatsoever ye shall ask the Father in my name, *which is right,* believing that ye shall receive, behold it shall be given unto you." (3 Nephi 18:20. Italics added.)

"Whatsoever ye ask the Father in my name it shall be given unto you, *that is expedient for you."* (D&C 88:64. Italics added.)

It seems that some people read the Lord's promise contained in the first scripture above and assume that through their prayers of faith, desired blessings will be claimed automatically. They may assume that what they are requesting is *right* or *expedient,* and that all they need to do is voice the prayer. This assumption would be proper and correct if the petitioner were completely righteous, completely in harmony with the Spirit, inspired to know fully the will of the Lord, and inclined to ask for that which is not contrary to God's will.

Would that all of us were worthy to receive the blessing pronounced upon Nephi, the son of Helaman:

"Blessed art thou, Nephi, for those things which thou hast done; for I have beheld how thou hast with unwearyingness declared the word, which I have given unto thee, unto this people. And thou has not feared them, and hast not sought thine own life, but *hast sought my will,* and to keep my commandments.

"And now, because thou hast done this with such unwearyingness, behold, I will bless thee forever; and I will make thee mighty in word and in deed, in faith and in works; yea, even that all things shall be done unto thee according to thy word, *for thou shalt not ask that which is contrary to my will."* (Helaman 10:4-5. Italics added.)

The promise to all of us is: ". . . if ye are purified and cleansed from all sin, ye shall ask whatsoever you will in the name of Jesus and it shall be done. But know this, it shall be given you what you shall ask." (D&C 50:29-30.)

"In My Name"

In answer to a question posed by Thomas, Jesus said: "I am the way, the truth, and the life: no man cometh unto the

Father, but by me." (John 14:6.) While instructing the Nephites, following his resurrection, he said: ". . . Ye must always pray unto the Father *in my name.*" (3 Nephi 18:19. Italics
added.) And, in modern times the Lord has declared: ". . .
Thou shalt continue in calling upon God *in my name.*" (D&C
24:5. Italics added.)

From the very beginning, even in the days of Adam, man
has received this direction: "Wherefore, thou shalt do all that
thou doest in the name of the Son, and thou shalt repent and
call upon God in the name of the Son forever." (Moses 5:8.)
President Marion G. Romney has said:

"Associated with belief in God, the Eternal Father, is
belief in his Son Jesus Christ and an acceptance of his divine
mission as the Redeemer of the world. This belief is as basic to
true prayer as is belief in God, the Eternal Father. It is because
Jesus is our Redeemer, and therefore our advocate with the
Father, that we must always pray unto the Father in his name.
Our hearts are filled with gratitude beyond expression for
what the Savior has done for us. We sing with feeling, 'Oh, it
is wonderful that he should care for me, enough to die for
me!' Every time we partake of the sacrament, we witness unto
the Father that we are willing to take upon us the name of his
Son. *A prayer not offered in his name suggests insincerity or lack of
understanding.*" (*Look to God and Live*, pp. 201-2. Italics added.)

We should end our prayers by asking in the name of Jesus
Christ. However, we should not close by saying, "In thy
name." This is confusing and raises the question, whose
name? the Father's or the Son's?

Amen

In accord with the Savior's pattern, all prayers are concluded with the word *Amen*. This word is used to express
solemn ratification, acceptance, or hearty approval. When a
person says "Amen" at the end of a prayer, he binds himself,
in a sense, to the words spoken.

Prayers spoken in behalf of a group should express the
thinking, needs, and desires of all, not just the individual serving as voice. Hopefully, the person who speaks for the group
has given prior thought to the assignment and has the spirit of
the occasion. Then, at the conclusion of the prayer, the

speaker's "Amen" is a signal for all to give an audible response. This combined "Amen" shows that the members of the group agree with the prayer and are party to what has been pronounced.

Hallowed language

A few years ago the question was asked: "Is it important that we use the words, thy, thine, thee, and thou, in addressing Deity; or is it proper when directing our thoughts in prayer to use the more common and modern words, you and yours?" President Joseph Fielding Smith provided this direct answer:

"Our Eternal Father and his Only Begotten Son, Jesus Christ, should never be approached in prayer in the familiar expressions so commonly used in addressing human beings. The Father and the Son should always be honored in our prayers in the utmost humility and reverence." Then President Smith added: "The changing of the wording of the Bible to meet the popular language of our day, has, in the opinion of the writer and his brethren, been a great loss in the building of faith and spirituality in the minds and hearts of the people." (*Answers to Gospel Questions*, Deseret Book Co., 1958, 2:15, 17.)

Another modern prophet, President Spencer W. Kimball, has written: "In all our prayers, it is well to use the pronouns *thee, thou, thy,* and *thine* instead of *you, your,* and *yours* inasmuch as they have come to indicate respect." (*Faith Precedes the Miracle*, Deseret Book Co., 1972, p. 201.)

In the general priesthood meeting, October 6, 1951, President Stephen L Richards remarked:

"We have discovered . . . a lack of proper teaching with reference to prayer. I know that I myself have been shocked as I have heard missionaries called on for prayer who seem to have had no experience or training whatever in the use of the language of prayer.

". . . I think, my brethren, that in the quorums and in the classes, you would do well, as in the homes, also, to teach the language of prayer—'thee' and 'thou' rather than 'you.' It always seems disappointing to me to have our Father in Heaven, our Lord, addressed as 'you.' It is surprising how much we see of this. . . . I think you might make a note of it, and avail yourselves of any opportunities that come in order to teach the sacred and reverential language of prayer."

We not only worship the true and living God, but we also bear witness to the world of his reality. Therefore, our worship and witness must build in the minds and hearts of men respect and reverence for God. We must approach him with awe, humility, and reverence, and invite others to do the same. Our language of prayer should be hallowed language that mirrors accuracy of faith and unquestioned respect and devotion to Deity.

Vain repetitions

"But when ye pray," the Savior taught, "use not vain repetitions, as the heathen do: for they think that they shall be heard for their much speaking. Be not ye therefore like unto them: for your Father knoweth what things ye have need of, before ye ask him." (Matthew 6:7-8.) This was strict warning against the overuse of idle, empty, or hollow expressions. Sometimes we speak without thinking and resort to the use of meaningless or threadbare terms. Sometimes we are tempted to parrot sweet-sounding or clever words coined by others. Such practices should be avoided.

President Ezra Taft Benson suggests: "Our prayers should be meaningful and pertinent. Do not use the same phrases at each prayer. Each of us would become disturbed if a friend said the same words to us each day, treated the conversation as a chore, and could hardly wait to finish in order to turn on the TV and forget us." (Ezra Taft Benson, *God, Family, Country*, Deseret Book Co., 1974, pp. 121-22.)

Length of prayers

There may be valid reasons and suitable circumstances for lengthy prayers. A dedication prayer might appropriately be longer than usual prayers. Yet we should normally avoid wordy or ear-tickling exercises of worship. Well might we remember these words: "Woe unto you, scribes and Pharisees, hypocrites! for ye devour widow's houses, and *for a pretence make long prayer*: therefore ye shall receive the greater damnation." (Matthew 23:14. Italics added.) Neither pretense nor hypocrisy has place in our conversations with God and man.

A number of years ago, Elder Francis M. Lyman had this to say about length of prayers: "It is not necessary to offer very long and tedious prayers, either at opening or closing. It is not only not pleasing to the Lord for us to use excess of words, but also it is not pleasing to the Latter-day Saints. Two minutes will open any kind of meeting, and a half minute will close it. . . . Offer short prayers, and avoid vain repetitions. . . ." (From an address delivered in MIA conference, June 5, 1892, and reprinted in *Improvement Era*, April 1947, p. 245.)

It is expected that invocations are longer and fuller in expression. We normally invoke the Spirit of the Lord (not a portion of it) to be with us, and we attempt to set the spiritual tone of the gathering. On the other hand, dismissal prayers are short and to the point. Thanks may appropriately be expressed for the spiritual upliftment of the occasion and blessings sought upon the point of departure.

I fear that in some of our meetings prayers have a tendency to be drawn out and full of trite or vain expressions. This tendency discourages participation in prayer, especially among the youth, and promotes clock-watching. How much better it would be if we prayed as the Nephites. It was said of them: ". . . and they did not multiply many words, for it was given unto them what they should pray, and they were filled with desire." (3 Nephi 19:24.)

More than mere words

Elder James E. Talmage wrote: "It is well to know that prayer is not compounded of words, words that may fail to express what one desires to say, words that so often cloak inconsistencies, words that may have no deeper source than the physical organs of speech, words that may be spoken to impress mortal ears. The dumb may pray, and that too with the eloquence that prevails in heaven. Prayer is made up of heart throbs and the righteous yearnings of the soul, of supplication based on the realization of need, of contrition and pure desire." (*Jesus the Christ*, p. 238.)

I suspect that some of the most acceptable prayers ever offered heavenward have been offered by those limited in language skills. The prayers of children are spoken simply; the prayers of the deaf are silent movements of the hands; the prayers of the handicapped may consist of only a pleading eye and look of innocence. But such prayers often transcend in beauty and import the wordy, complicated soundings of a pseudoscholar.

I remember with extreme fondness the prayers of Sister Berta Piranian, the wife of my mission president, Badwagon Piranian. Sister Piranian's native tongue was German; English, her second language, was not so polished. When she prayed or bore her testimony in English it was broken, simple, and dotted with grammatical errors. Still, her prayers were so beautiful and so reflective of her goodness. No one who ever heard those prayers doubted her ability to communicate with Deity.

These comments are not intended to imply that we should not seek eloquence and excellence of language in our prayers. We should seek perfection in our prayers as we seek perfection in other aspects of our living and worship. However, these comments are made to establish the fact that true eloquence is found in the feeling that accompanies the words. An acceptable prayer is more than mere words.

Shakespeare's play *Hamlet* includes these words of Claudius when he broke off praying because his heart was not in it: "My words fly up, my thoughts remain below; / Words without thoughts never to heaven go." (Act III, sc. 3.)

The Master spoke these plain words that should not be overlooked: "This people draweth nigh unto me with their mouth, and honoureth me with their lips; but their heart is far from me." (Matthew 15:8.)

Conclusion

In conclusion, here is a summary of standards for prayer. These guidelines provide the basic do's and don'ts relating to the approved form and accepted language of prayer:

1. *Salutations.* Prayers are addressed to "Our Father which art in heaven." As we pray to our Father in heaven, we should avoid using the term "Lord." We should also avoid the unnecessary repetition of the name of Deity.

2. *Expressions of thanks.* Prayers may appropriately contain expressions of praise and thanksgiving, such as, "I thank thee

that . . ." and "I thank thee for. . . ." In public prayer, we speak for the entire group and use the pronouns *we* and *ours*, never *I* or *my*.

3. *Petitions.* Prayers may appropriately include requests or petitions for divine assistance, forgiveness of sin, inspiration, etc., such as "I pray thee that thou wilt. . . ." We must be willing to subject our petitions to the will of our Father in heaven ("Not my will, but thine, be done"). We should live righteously so we will know what is right and expedient for us, and so we will not ask for that which is contrary to God's will.

4. *"In my name."* Prayers are made or done in the name of Jesus Christ, for he has instructed, "Ye must always pray unto the Father in my name." We should not close by saying, "In *thy* name."

5. *Amen.* Prayers are concluded with the word *Amen,* which expresses acceptance or approval. We should say "Amen" aloud when we are in a group and someone prays in behalf of that group.

6. *Hallowed language.* Prayers are spoken in the sacred language of prayer (that of the King James Version of the Bible). We should use the reverent words *thy, thine, thee,* and *thou* in addressing Deity. We should not resort to the popular language of the day and use the common pronouns *you, your,* and *yours.*

7. *Vain repetitions.* Prayers should be meaningful and pertinent. We do not use vain repetitions, such as the repeated use of the name of Deity. We also avoid the use of idle, meaningless, threadbare terms and expressions.

8. *Length of prayers.* Prayers should be suited to the occasion and offered in a concise, honest manner. We should not "for a pretence make long prayers" or become involved in wordy or ear-tickling exercises of worship. Invocations are normally longer and fuller in expression. In such prayers we invoke the Spirit of the Lord (not a portion of it) to be with us. Dismissal prayers are normally short and to the point.

9. *More than mere words.* Prayers are the "heart throbs and the righteous yearnings of the soul." We should seek eloquence and excellence of language in our communion with God. However, we should understand that true eloquence in prayer is found in the feeling that accompanies the words.

Remember, "Prayers . . . are expected to conform to a prescribed standard of divine excellence; they should fit into the approved pattern of proper prayer." (Elder Bruce R. McConkie, *op. cit.*) ". . . we ought not to make too much of form. The Lord rules against long and hypocritical prayers." (President Spencer W. Kimball, *op. cit.*, pp. 201-2.) We should also avoid set or memorized prayers, except in the case of prescribed baptismal and sacramental prayers that have fixed meaning.

A few years ago, while serving as a mission president, I determined that I would begin a series of interviews with the missionaries by asking, "When did you have your last spiritual experience?" The replies were varied and revealing. Some confessed that they had not experienced anything special. Others said that it had been some time since they had felt a closeness to the Spirit. Still others told me of marvelous experiences that had occurred the day or days previous to the interview. One missionary's answer, however, was unique. His response was, "This morning." "This morning?" I repeated. "What happened this morning?" Slowly, yet confidently, he replied, "I prayed." I was thrilled by the missionary's response. I did not doubt his word, for I knew of his commitment, his spiritual nature, and his ability to pray.

Many times since this experience I have pondered the matter of prayer and spiritual experiences. I've concluded only that which is obvious—our dialogue with Deity can and ought to be very special and very uplifting. And it can be if we seek God humbly and sincerely. We must approach him with childlike faith and we must pray in a Christlike way.

I pray that we will follow the true pattern of prayer and employ the reverent and sacred language of prayer. Would that it could be said of our prayers as it was said of the Savior's: "The eye hath never seen, neither hath the ear heard, before, so great and marvelous things as we saw and heard Jesus speak unto the Father;

"And no tongue can speak, neither can there be written by any man, neither can the hearts of men conceive so great and marvelous things as we both saw and heard Jesus speak; and no one can conceive of the joy which filled our souls at the time we heard him pray for us unto the Father." (3 Nephi 17:16-17.)

WHAT SHOULD
WE PRAY FOR?

Elder Neal A. Maxwell

There are so many instructive
examples of prayer in the scriptures! The very variety of examples requires us to sort out the strategic things with regard to
the purposes of our petitions and the content of our prayers.

In the Book of Mormon we read that the Savior directed,
"Whatsoever ye shall ask the Father in my name, *which is
right*, believing that ye shall receive, behold it shall be given
unto you." (3 Nephi 18:20. Italics added.)

This is one of the most significant and distinctive insights
given to us in all of the scriptures. Even though we may ask in
faith for something, unless it is right for us, God reserves the
decision-making power to himself. A perfect, loving, and
omniscient Father would do just that. Thus, in addition to
having faith, we need to ask for that which is right. This same
tonal truth appears in modern revelations. The Lord told the
Prophet Joseph Smith, "Whatsoever ye ask the Father in my
name, it shall be given unto you, that is *expedient* for you."
(D&C 88:64. Italics added.)

Clearly, the Lord reserves the right to determine that
which is best for us, lest we ask for something in our spiritual
naiveté that would not conform to the will of God. Nephi, the
prophet, understood the importance of precision and propriety in prayer. He knew from happy experience that God
would give liberally to him if he, Nephi, prayed in such a way
that he "ask not amiss." (2 Nephi 4:35.)

Thus we see the importance of what a modern prophet has
told us. President Joseph F. Smith asserted that spiritual
growth includes "the education of our desires." Our task is to
come to that point in our progress where our very desires are
right in the sight of God. When we arrive at that point, we
will have the "mind of Christ." (1 Corinthians 2:16.) From
those with the "mind of Christ" will come perfect prayers.

Continuing to speak of strategic things, we must have the
Spirit with us, so that the Holy Ghost can prompt us to pray

for that which is right. Nephi advised us that the Spirit "teacheth a man to pray." (2 Nephi 32:8.) There is, therefore, a definite connection between our righteousness and our capacity to draw upon the Spirit so that we will ask for what we should ask for. The Lord told Joseph Smith in 1831, "And if ye are purified and cleansed from all sin, ye shall ask whatsoever you will in the name of Jesus, and it shall be done. But know this, it shall be *given* you what you shall ask. . . ." (D&C 50:29-30. Italics added.)

Obviously this purposeful praying reflects a high order of spirituality. For those of us less far along in the path of prayer, these insights at first might seem quite discouraging, because while the promises are valid, we feel so distant from that point when "it shall be given you what you shall ask." Even so, we need to understand the significance of these scriptures if we are to move very far along the path of prayer by learning to pray for correct things as well as developing our faith. Only then will our prayers deserve to be characterized as counseling "with the Lord in all [our] doings." (Alma 37:37.)

One might ask, Why is it necessary that the Holy Ghost prompt us even in our prayers? One reason is that only with the help of the Holy Ghost can we be lifted outside the narrow little theater of our own experience, outside our selfish concerns, and outside the confines of our tiny conceptual cells. It was Jacob who reminded us, and in such beautiful language, that the Spirit (which teaches us to pray) also "speaketh of things as they really are, and of things as they really will be." (Jacob 4:13.) The Spirit "searcheth . . . the deep things of God" (1 Corinthians 2:10), and superficial prayer will not produce such probings.

God sees things as they really are and as they will become. We don't! In order to tap that precious perspective during our prayers, we must rely upon the promptings of the Holy Ghost. With access to that kind of knowledge, we would then pray for what we and others should have—*really* have. With the Spirit prompting us, we will not ask "amiss."

With access to the Spirit, our circles of concern will expand. The mighty prayer of Enos began with understandable self-concern, moved outward to family, then to his enemies, and then outward to future generations.

Lest one become prematurely discouraged because of the

less lofty patterns in his own prayers, we can grow in experience in prayer as in all things. The Prophet Joseph Smith on one occasion said, "A person may profit by noticing the first intimation of the spirit of revelation; for instance, when you feel pure intelligence flowing into you, it may give you sudden strokes of ideas, so that by noticing it, . . . you may grow into the principle of revelation, until you become perfect in Christ Jesus." (*Teachings of the Prophet Joseph Smith,* p. 151.) When our prayers are inspired, we actually learn from our very petitions, just as President Marion G. Romney has observed that when he speaks under inspiration, he learns from what he says.

To be able to tap divine perspective, with regard to the content of our petitions, thus becomes exceedingly important. Otherwise we might pray for a job that wouldn't be right for us. We might ask "amiss" in terms of removing a challenge before us, when what we need is help in order to cope with that challenge. There are ever so many ways in which we must come to be guided even in the content of our prayers. It is not enough to kneel, important as that is, or to have faith, as essential as that is. We must come to bend our will to the will of God, so that in our prayers we really commune with him and ask for those things which are right.

The Lord has told us with regard to truth, and presumably this would include truths about ourselves and our own circumstances—the very things about which we pray so often—that "truth is knowledge of things as they are, and as they were, and as they are to come." (D&C 93:24.) This connection of the past with present circumstances and with the future provides a convergence of truth that can give us precious perspective about ourselves and our circumstances. Such perspective would undoubtedly alter the objects of our sometimes petty petitions or narrow and naive requests to our Heavenly Father. Hopefully, we will never forget that "all things . . . past, present, and future . . . are continually before the Lord." (D&C 130:7.)

Meanwhile, it should not cause dismay in ourselves or others that there are gradations of spiritual perceptivity. People can witness the same phenomenon and understand it in varying degrees. In one of his marvelous prayers, Jesus prayed with such earnestness and power that "then came there a voice of heaven," referring to the glorification of the name of God. When the voice of heaven came, the scriptures tell us, "the people therefore that stood by, and heard it, said that it thundered: others said, An angel spake to him. Jesus answered and said, This voice came not because of me, but for your sakes." (John 12:28-29.) Perhaps there were some who heard nothing at all; some who heard the sound but thought it to be thunder; some who recognized it as a voice but did not understand the words; some who thought it was the voice of an angel; and some who knew it was the voice of God.

Having said these strategic things, let us now look at what we learn in the scriptures about proper prayers, so far as the content of these petitions is concerned.

The obvious tactical truths are that we can appropriately pray for many things: for forgiveness, for strength, for direction over our daily affairs, for leaders, for family, and for mankind. We also ought to have as the purpose of some prayers sheer adoration. But having generalized, let us examine the record for appropriate models.

Moses, when Israel had sinned, was asked by his people to "pray unto the Lord, that he take away the serpents from us." Under these circumstances "Moses prayed for the people." (Numbers 21:7.) It is significant that Moses prayed for the people in spite of the fact that many of them were unworthy of the practical blessing they sought; they failed to take advantage of the instrument (the brass serpent upon the pole) that was provided so that if they were bitten by the fiery serpents they had only to look in order to be healed. Moses prayed anyway.

In the Book of Mormon we find a striking insight into a somewhat parallel circumstance in which Mormon prayed for the people but acknowledged that it was a prayer "without faith," because of the exceeding wickedness of the people. However, Mormon kept praying. (Mormon 3:12.)

It is also appropriate for us to pray for leaders and for helpers. Jesus did this in praying for his disciples. Significantly he said, "I pray not that thou shouldest take them out of the world, but that thou shouldest keep them from the evil." (John 17:15.) The Lord did not ask for an exemption for his followers. Praying for others that they shall overcome indicates that all temptation and trials are not to be removed from our pathway. Prayers are not to be bulldozers that automatically clear the way of all roadblocks.

In the Book of Mormon, Jesus instructed his followers to pray for their wives and children. (3 Nephi 18:21.) We should do so—and by name—so that our family members hear themselves being prayed over.

Obviously, we should pray when leaders are being selected. In Samuel's selection of Saul, under the inspiration of heaven, we read of the systematic search for a new king. It was work—real work—as family after family came before Samuel. Upon inquiring of the Lord, the Lord indicated that the man to be crowned "hath hid himself." The people ran and fetched Saul, "and when he stood among the people, he was higher than any of the people from his shoulders and upward." (1 Samuel 10:22-23.) Virtually every weekend, General Authorities of the Church pray, for instance, as men are chosen to preside over stakes. It is an appropriate object of prayer; indeed, it is a necessity.

We know that the Prophet Joseph Smith prayed for forgiveness of his sins. He said on one occasion, "I betook myself to prayer and supplication to Almighty God for forgiveness of all my sins and folly, and also for a manifestation to me, that I might know of my state and standing before him. . . ." (Joseph Smith 2:29.) Surely each of us has many occasions when such petitions are necessary.

Daniel was esteemed. The scriptures tell us that "an excellent spirit was in him." (Daniel 6:3.) He apparently prayed on his knees at least three times a day, facing Jerusalem and giving thanks before his God. Daniel's prayers were prayers of thanksgiving, were sincere, and were regularized before he was placed in the den of lions. It is significant that King Darius, who had reluctantly placed Daniel in that den of lions, fasted for Daniel's safety and "slept not"! Regularity in praying does not mean that our prayers must be ritualized or become routine.

The object of some prayers is more obvious, though still not inappropriate, than others. Some objects are apt to be subtle and soul-stretching. For instance, one of the ways of testing ourselves is to ask ourselves how often we have actually followed the injunction from the Savior in which he said that we should pray for those who despitefully use us and persecute us. (Matthew 5:44.) How often have we specifically prayed for those who use, abuse, manipulate, and exploit us?

How often do we praise the Lord "with a prayer of praise and thanksgiving"? (D&C 136:28.) As noted earlier, some prayers ought to be prayers of sheer adoration. Adoration, absent of any petition, even occasionally would be a better mix than prayers that are perpetual petitions and relentless requests, minus adoration and appreciation.

Close examination of the Lord's Prayer (using the models given us in the New Testament and in the Book of Mormon) indicates the need for reverent salutation as we open the prayer; our expressed desire that the work and the will of God be accomplished; a request for our daily bread (not for an annuity or pension); a petition for reciprocal forgiveness (it would be wrong to pray for forgiveness unless we have a forgiving spirit ourselves); a desire to avoid temptation or to be delivered from evil; an indication of submission in which we acknowledge that the kingdom is God's and the glory is his.

On our own small scale we can, as Jesus did, pray that certain "cups" will pass from us. But we must also do as he did by saying, "Nevertheless, not as I will, but as thou wilt." (Matthew 26:39.)

We can pray as Jesus did in his great high priestly prayer (John 17) in which he actually reviews his stewardship with a loving Father in heaven; he also prayed for his disciples, and for unity.

How often have we reviewed our stewardship in like manner, especially vocally? How appropriate that Jesus reviewed his stewardship just before the betrayal.

We can and should pray for effectiveness in our ministry so we will be able to speak God's word with effectiveness, whether as a Primary teacher or a missionary or whatever. The saints assembled after Jesus' ascension did so when they said, "Grant unto thy servants, that with all boldness they may speak thy word." Following this prayer "they were all filled with the Holy Ghost, and they spake the word of God with boldness." Significantly, when there was such communion and selflessness in prayer, "the multitude of them that believed were *of one heart* and of one soul." (Acts 4:29, 31-32. Italics added.)

Paul urged us to "let [our] requests be known unto God

. . . by prayer and supplication with thanksgiving." (Philippians 4:6.) In the Book of Mormon, we are instructed to pray over our fields and over our flocks. And elsewhere in the Book of Mormon we are told to "counsel with the Lord in all [our] doings." (Alma 37:37.) God will think nothing trivial if it bears upon our salvation. God never holds us in contempt. He smiles upon us, but never laughs at the childishness of our prayers, though we have an obligation to grow in the effectiveness of them.

Can we pray for inappropriate things? Of course we can. We can pray for wickedness *with* happiness; for status *and* humility. The Lord said that Martin Harris was not to trouble him further. (D&C 5:26-28.) There is a difference between pressing the Lord for something that is not right and importuning for something that is right. The test is the rightness of the request, not the span of time over which it is made. Protracted petitions (even when right) may be required, since persistence is sometimes necessary for us to grow.

We need to pray for confirmation of decisions we are about to make, noting that we are first to study it out in our minds. (D&C 9:8.) Some of us in our laziness attempt to use God as a research assistant.

What then might be said of the topical blocks, the common blocks, that get in our way when we struggle over what to pray for? First, there is a lack of realization on our part that we can actually be guided in terms of what we should pray for. We tend to *pour out* petitions without letting inspiration *pour in*. God can truly prompt us in our prayers to ask for that which is right to not ask amiss. God can educate our desires.

We also sometimes fail to study things out in our mind before praying so that we do not fully frame our questions and petitions. Our petitions are often skimpy on the "whereas" and move too quickly to the "be it resolved" portion of prayer. Further, we sometimes deflect the promptings that come when we petition; these may be faint beginnings of our apprenticeship in prayer and in revelation.

We may sometimes inappropriately pray, in effect, to be taken out of the world rather than praying that we will be kept from evil and prevail.

We too often pray in generalities rather than specifics. A vague prayer is hardly a prayer at all.

We may be too embarrassed to bring before the Lord specific weaknesses we have, yet he knows of them anyway. We thus prevent ourselves from gathering and gaining the strength we might need to overcome them. Admitting aloud (though in private) our weaknesses and stating our promises is sometimes better than just thinking of them. Dealing with our specific weaknesses is far better than simply praying that we will be more righteous.

Fatigue tends to produce prayers that are hasty generalities. This suggests that to pray only just before retirement at the end of a taxing day is to adversely affect the content of our prayers.

Our unwillingness to deal boldly with our own problems tends to produce prayers in which the objects of the petitions are couched again in generalities.

Other chapters elsewhere in this book speak of other dimensions of prayer, but presumably, as with Enos, we could, if needed and prepared, engage "in mighty prayer" over many hours. Meanwhile, most of us should improve the quality of our briefer prayers. That would be a beginning. And in the beginning men began "to call upon the name of the Lord." (Genesis 4:26.) Without proper purpose we sometimes pray just so we can be seen or heard praying. Verily, we have our reward when people thus see or hear us pray. Surely we should expect no further reward from such vain prayer. The Savior referred to those who pray in this manner as hypocrites. (Matthew 6:5-8.) Vain repetition also obstructs, perhaps more than repetition *per se*, but we must beware well-worn phrases which denote laziness rather than freshness.

Finally, if we need to consult someone concerning the content of our prayers, we would do well to consult our conscience. By consulting our conscience, the obvious would assert itself, and the inappropriate content in prayer could disappear. We may pray and plead for someone to understand us, when (under the doctrine of Matthew 18:15) it is up to us to take the initiative in seeking out that person to end the impasse. Conscience can call us to account such tactical matters.

There is a real risk that praying, therefore, for wrong things (or things which at least are not right) will immobilize us or leave us on a lower performance plateau, so that we never scale the heights to which real prayer could take us.

We are given an ultimate and stunning promise that takes us back to the opening paragraphs of this chapter. The Lord promises us, "He that asketh in the Spirit asketh *according to the will of God; wherefore it is done even as he asketh.*" (D&C 46:30. Italics added.) What power! What proximity!

It is out of the depths of true prayer that an individual rises to real heights. When Jesus "fell on his face," in prayer he drew close to the throne of his loving Father, and he thus drew strength to complete his divine mission "according to the will of God."

KNOWING
AND ACCEPTING
ANSWERS
TO PRAYER

Elder L. Tom Perry

I have always been grateful I was blessed to be reared in a home where we were taught to appreciate the value of prayer. My earliest recollection as a child was kneeling at the knee of my mother each night as we retired. This was her training ground to teach us how to pray. As simple words and sentences were repeated for her hearing, quiet whispers from her lips would often be heard to remind us to make our prayer one of gratitude.

Our family consisted of our parents and six children. The three oldest were girls and the three youngest were boys. My brothers and I shared the same bedroom. As we advanced in age we graduated from prayers at Mother's knee to personal prayers at our bedside. Mother continued to supervise the process until she was certain we were sufficiently mature to handle it on our own. As we retired, we always had a consciousness of the nearness of Mother. She would stand outside our door until the right combination of sounds verified the fact that her sons had been on their knees to thank the Lord for his blessings of that day. If we were forgetful we would hear her voice, "Boys, have you said your prayers?" If we had remembered, then after prayers were completed and we jumped into bed, we would hear her footsteps going downstairs to complete her day's activities.

Mother assumed the responsibility each morning of turning the backs of the chairs toward the table as a reminder to have family prayers before partaking of the first nourishment of the day. How we enjoyed hearing our father pour out his heart to the Lord asking for the protection of his family! It was as if a special shield had been placed around us by a father bearing the priesthood as we would embark on our daily activities at the beginning of each day.

We were blessed with a father who understood the power of prayer. When I was growing up, the family home evening program was not as formal as it is today with Monday nights set aside for that special purpose. Our family was in the habit of gathering together several nights each week to play games and be instructed by Father. He was a master storyteller. We especially enjoyed hearing stories of his early life as a boy and a young man. He had a very effective way of weaving in a special lesson with each story.

Our favorite stories were those of a unique opportunity Father had to earn his way through high school. Upon approaching high-school age, he was troubled with the decision of whether to remain on the farm to assist his father or to seek an education. Attending high school would require leaving home, because there were no schools in that farm area. The family was poor and without the means of providing assistance to the children interested in continuing their schooling. My father had the courage and determination to leave home and seek an education. His father agreed to assist him all he could. This consisted of a one-way ticket to Salt Lake City and five dollars to get started. With this, Father left his home.

Upon his arrival in Salt Lake City, he immediately found it necessary to find employment. Even in those days five dollars would not last long. He heard of a job opportunity at the Beehive House and decided to apply for the position. Much to his shock and surprise, he was interviewed by the wife of the President of the Church, who at that time was President Joseph F. Smith.

Father's many years of experience milking cows qualified him for the position, and he was employed by the prophet's family. Fringe benefits included board and room at the Beehive House. His journal records how the Smith family took him in and treated him as if he were a member of the family.

He would tell us what a special thrill it was to hear President Smith pray as they knelt together as a family in prayer each morning and evening. He would add there was never any doubt that the prophet conversed with the Lord in family prayer.

The prophet would counsel his children not to pray for gifts, but for opportunities. If the Lord just opened the windows of heaven and poured gifts on the heads of his children, there would be no growth and development. But if he was kind enough to provide them with opportunities, then as they took advantage of that which he had provided for them they would grow with the power of achievement.

These special lessons taught by President Smith to his family and repeated by my father to his family impressed on us the power of daily communications with our Father in heaven. As we added to these early instructions study of the scriptures, our capacity to understand the purpose and meaning of prayer became greatly multiplied in our lives. It was established on a firm foundation.

Armed with this special understanding and training on what to expect from prayers, it has been easy for me to establish confidence in the Lord that if I will make the effort to study a problem out in my own mind and then present my determined course to him for ratification, he will respond with a burning of acceptance or a stupor of thought as rejection.

The account of Oliver Cowdery and his request to have an opportunity to translate in addition to being a scribe, as he and the Prophet Joseph worked together on the writing of the Book of Mormon, has always given me a greater understanding of how the Lord works with his children.

It has been my personal experience if we will work things out in our own minds, ask in faith, and be prepared to accept the direction we receive, the Lord will not deny us answers to our prayers.

The Savior in his Sermon on the Mount taught his disciples how to pray. After giving them instruction on the form to be used, he said:

"Therefore take no thought, saying, What shall we eat? or, What shall we drink? or, Wherewithal shall we be clothed?

"(For after all these things do the Gentiles seek:) for your Heavenly Father knoweth that ye have need of all these things.

"But seek ye first the kingdom of God, and his righteousness; and all these things shall be added unto you." (Matthew 6:31-33.)

I have complete faith in the power of prayer. I have confidence that answers are received if we are willing to make our petitions in righteousness and accept fully the direction we receive from the Lord. "The ways of the Lord are right." (Hosea 14:9.)

SACRED,
SET PRAYERS

Elder Mark E. Petersen

By revelation the Lord has given the Church three set prayers for use in our sacred ordinances. Except for these prayers, the Lord seems to expect us to express ourselves in our own words as we approach him in supplication.

All three of these revealed prayers relate to the atonement of the Lord Jesus Christ, his crucifixion, and his burial and resurrection. All of the ordinances in which we use these prayers place us under solemn covenants of obedience to God. They are the sacrament of the Lord's Supper and the ordinance of baptism.

The atonement of the Savior was the most sacred event of all time. It was the zenith of all mortal experience. All life is focused upon it. Our eternal progression is made possible through it.

Because we are the children of God, our Heavenly Father has granted us the privilege of eventually becoming like him and has provided a plan whereby this may be accomplished. We finite mortals cannot comprehend the extent of such an infinite blessing, for we still see through a glass darkly and understand imperfectly. But this we know: We are the children of God, and it is possible for us to become like him. However, without the atonement of the Savior, such a goal would not be attainable, for the atonement is the gateway to this great opportunity.

As children of God we were assembled in a grand council in our preexistent life and there had explained to us the privileges that our Father proposed should be ours. When we heard his plan, "the morning stars sang together, and all the sons of God shouted for joy." (Job 38:7.)

It was made plain that this was an essential step in our eternal progress; that we would come to earth under mortal conditions that would test us and try us, and that opposites would confront us, enticing us either toward the good or the evil. The reality of sin would face us. Physical death would be our lot.

If allowed to continue unchecked, both sin and death would forever prevent us from becoming like God. It was essential, therefore, that we be saved from both. But such a saving procedure would require the services of a Savior so powerful that he could conquer sin and destroy death.

In that pre-earth council, Jehovah was chosen as our Savior. The Lord revealed this great event to Moses in these words:

"And I, the Lord God, spake unto Moses, saying: That Satan, whom thou hast commanded in the name of mine Only Begotten, is the same which was from the beginning, and he came before me, saying—Behold, here am I, send me, I will be thy son, and I will redeem all mankind, that one soul shall not be lost, and surely I will do it; wherefore give me thine honor.

"But, behold, my Beloved Son, which was my Beloved and Chosen from the beginning, said unto me—Father, thy will be done, and the glory be thine forever.

"Wherefore, because that Satan rebelled against me, and sought to destroy the agency of man, which I, the Lord God, had given him, and also, that I should give unto him mine own power; by the power of mine Only Begotten, I caused that he should be cast down;

"And he became Satan, yea, even the devil, the father of all lies, to deceive and to blind men, and to lead them captive at his will, even as many as would not hearken unto my voice." (Moses 4:1-4.)

Abraham added the following details:

"Now the Lord had shown unto me, Abraham, the intelligences that were organized before the world was; and among all these there were many of the noble and great ones;

"And God saw these souls that they were good, and he stood in the midst of them, and he said: These I will make my rulers; for he stood among those that were spirits, and he saw that they were good; and he said unto me: Abraham, thou art one of them; thou wast chosen before thou wast born.

"And there stood one among them that was like unto God, and he said unto those who were with him: We will go down, for there is space there, and we will take of these materials, and we will make an earth whereon these may dwell;

"And we will prove them herewith, to see if they will do all things whatsoever the Lord their God shall command them;

"And they who keep their first estate shall be added upon; and they who keep not their first estate shall not have glory in the same kingdom with those who keep their first estate; and they who keep their second estate shall have glory added upon their heads for ever and ever.

"And the Lord said: Whom shall I send? And one answered like unto the Son of Man: Here am I, send me. And another answered and said: Here am I, send me. And the Lord said: I will send the first.

"And the second was angry, and kept not his first estate, and, at that day, many followed after him." (Abraham 3:22-28.)

No human mind can measure the vast significance of the selection of Jehovah as our Savior. Without his sacrifice all mortals would have been permanent subjects of the devil, and our bodies would forever remain in the tomb, never again to rise, for there would be no resurrection. Without his atonement we never could become like our Father in heaven.

But through the gracious act of Jehovah, the most beloved son of God, all our promised progress became possible. He expressed his own complete willingness to become a vicarious offering for us, first to break the grip of sin, and then to overcome death and bring about a glorious resurrection of our bodies. So it is that through his grace we can rise above our fallen state, receive redemption from the grave, and move into eternity, there to continue to work toward becoming like our Heavenly Father.

The Savior was the creator of the universes and provided this earth as a mortal home for us. When it was completed, the spirit children of God began to come here, taking on physical tabernacles, as the Lord had planned, and beginning the experience of mortality, being tested and tried, taught and enlightened, enticed by sin but also invited to an enjoyment of higher and better things by the power of the Holy Spirit.

In the meridian of time the Savior himself was born into mortality. The hosts of heaven understood the significance of his birth and made their joy manifest on that first Christmas night. The angels announced the great event to the shepherds, who then found the birthplace and worshiped the newborn King. The Wisemen learned of it, followed the new star, and brought gifts of gold, frankincense, and myrhh. But mankind generally was woefully unconscious of the most important birth ever to take place.

The Christ grew to manhood. At about thirty years of age he began his ministry. His call was: "The kingdom of God is at hand: repent ye, and believe the gospel." (Mark 1:15.)

And how important was that call to repentance! To earn the blessings of his atonement, all must respond to it. Without it there is no redemption from sin. The Savior explained this to the Prophet Joseph Smith:

"Therefore I command you to repent—repent, lest I smite you by the rod of my mouth, and by my wrath, and by my anger, and your sufferings be sore—how sore you know not, how exquisite you know not, yea, how hard to bear you know not.

"For behold, I, God have suffered these things for all, that they might not suffer if they would repent;

"But if they would not repent they must suffer even as I;

"Which suffering caused myself, even God, the greatest of all, to tremble because of pain, and to bleed at every pore, and to suffer both body and spirit—and would that I might not drink the bitter cup, and shrink—

"Nevertheless, glory be to the Father, and I partook and finished my preparations unto the children of men.

"Wherefore, I command you again to repent, lest I humble you with my almighty power; and that you confess your sins, lest you suffer these punishments of which I have spoken, of which in the smallest, yea, even in the least degree you have tasted at the time I withdrew my Spirit." (D&C 19:15-20.)

Remission of sins is provided for all who truly repent, but if we wilfully rebel against God, knowing the truth, and refuse to obey him, we forfeit our salvation. The prophet Abinadi explained it in this way:

"But behold, and fear, and tremble before God, for ye ought to tremble; for the Lord redeemeth none such that rebel against him and die in their sins; yea, even all those that have perished in their sins ever since the world began, that have wilfully rebelled against God, that have known the commandments of God, and would not keep them; these are they that have no part in the first resurrection.

"Therefore ought ye not to tremble? For salvation cometh to none such; for the Lord hath redeemed none such; yea, neither can the Lord redeem such; for he cannot deny himself; for he cannot deny justice when it has its claim." (Mosiah 15:26-27.)

The Lord gave us baptism as the means by which we obtain forgiveness of sins, and he explained the ordinance in these words:

"Verily I say unto you, that whoso repenteth of his sins through your words and desireth to be baptized in my name, on this wise shall ye baptize them—Behold, ye shall go down and stand in the water, and in my name shall ye baptize them.

"And now behold, these are the words which ye shall say, calling them by name, saying:

"Having authority given me of Jesus Christ, I baptize you in the name of the Father, and of the Son, and of the Holy Ghost. Amen.

"And then shall ye immerse them in the water, and come forth again out of the water.

"And after this manner shall ye baptize in my name; for behold, verily I say unto you, that the Father, and the Son, and the Holy Ghost are one; and I am in the Father, and the Father in me, and the Father and I are one." (3 Nephi 11:23-27.)

Baptism is our means of admission into the Lord's church and provides remission of sins so that we may enter his kingdom cleansed of our guilt. But it is even more than that. It is a constant reminder of the death, burial, and resurrection of the Lord Jesus Christ. It is administered with that very thought in mind. Therefore it must be performed by immersion.

In proper baptism we are buried in the water in the likeness of Christ's burial in the tomb. We come forth in the likeness of his resurrection from the tomb. Hence baptism becomes a symbol and a constant reminder of Christ's victory over death and of his assurance that all mankind will rise again, even as he did, physically and whole, for as in Adam all die, even so in Christ shall all be made alive. (1 Corinthians 15:22.)

Baptism then, as a symbol of this vital part of the Lord's atonement, becomes one of our most sacred and essential ordinances, one that the Lord himself has safeguarded against disputation (3 Nephi 11:28-30), against changes in the mode of its administration, and even against those who seek to eliminate it altogether.

Part of that safeguard is the divine prescription of the actual words to be said by the officiating priesthood holder. Not any words will do. The Lord did not leave this ceremony to the individual desires of any and all who might seek to perform it. Baptism is vital and unchangeable. It must be performed in the precise manner prescribed directly by revelation.

Since the whole procedure of baptism was so carefully and explicitly set forth by the Lord himself, it is not to be wondered at that he would give us the specific wording to be used as we immerse the candidate in the water. We usually speak of those words as a prayer, although they are stated more like a sacred declaration.

As the scripture explains:

"Baptism is to be administered in the following manner unto all those who repent—

"The person who is called of God and has authority from Jesus Christ to baptize, shall go down into the water with the person who has presented himself or herself for baptism, and shall say, calling him or her by name: Having been commissioned of Jesus Christ, I baptize you in the name of the Father, and of the Son, and of the Holy Ghost. Amen.

"Then shall he immerse him or her in the water, and come forth again out of the water." (D&C 20:72-74.)

Baptism thus administered becomes a covenant between the candidate and the Lord. In it we literally take upon ourselves the name of Christ, with all the responsibility thereto attached, and by the act of immersion we pledge to high heaven our "determination to serve him to the end." This is the covenant.

The scripture explains as follows:

"*And again, by way of commandment to the church concerning the manner of baptism*—All those who humble themselves before God, and desire to be baptized, and come forth with broken hearts and contrite spirits, and witness before the church that they have truly repented of all their sins, and are willing to take upon them the name of Jesus Christ, having a determination to serve him to the end, and truly manifest by their works that they have received of the Spirit of Christ unto the remission of their sins, shall be received by baptism into his church." (D&C 20:37.)

So baptism accomplishes these things:

1. Through it we recognize and accept the atoning sacrifice of the Savior.

2. By accepting baptism we "humble ourselves and come forth with broken hearts and contrite spirits" and manifest our complete repentance from all our sins, thus qualifying for the application of Christ's blood to cleanse us of our guilt.

3. We receive a remission of our sins thus repented of.

4. We take upon ourselves the name of Christ.

5. We determine to serve him the rest of our days.

6. We qualify for the ministrations of the Holy Spirit.

7. We become members of his church and kingdom here on earth.

And all of this is introduced by the few words provided by revelation, spoken by the officiating priesthood holder in the name of the Savior. Call it a prayer or a declaration, it nevertheless becomes a binding act.

The Lord's attitude toward remission of sins is further explained by the prophet Ezekiel:

"The soul that sinneth, it shall die. The son shall not bear the iniquity of the father, neither shall the father bear the iniquity of the son: the righteousness of the righteous shall be upon him, and the wickedness of the wicked shall be upon him.

"But if the wicked will turn from all his sins that he hath committed, and keep all my statutes, and do that which is lawful and right, he shall surely live, he shall not die.

"All his transgressions that he hath committed, they shall not be mentioned unto him: in his righteousness that he hath done he shall live.

"Have I any pleasure at all that the wicked should die? saith the Lord God: and not that he should return from his ways, and live?" (Ezekiel 18:20-23.)

However, the prophet also speaks of the unrepentant:

"But when the righteous turneth away from his righteousness, and committeth iniquity, and doeth according to all the abominations that the wicked man doeth, shall he live? All his righteousness that he hath done shall not be mentioned: in his trespass that he hath trespassed, and in his sin that he hath sinned, in them shall he die." (V. 24.)

In chapter 33 of Ezekiel we read further:

"Say unto them, As I live, saith the Lord God, I have no pleasure in the death of the wicked; but that the wicked turn from his way and live; turn ye, turn ye from your evil ways; for why will ye die, O house of Israel?

"Therefore, thou son of man, say unto the children of thy people, The righteousness of the righteous shall not deliver him in the day of his transgression: as for the wickedness of the wicked, he shall not fall thereby in the day that he turneth from his wickedness; neither shall the righteous be able to live for his righteousness in the day that he sinneth.

"When I shall say to the righteous, that he shall surely live; if he trust to his own righteousness, and commit iniquity, all his righteousnesses shall not be remembered; but for his iniquity that he hath committed, he shall die for it.

"Again, when I say unto the wicked, Thou shalt surely die; if he turn from his sin, and do that which is lawful and right;

"If the wicked restore the pledge, give again that he had robbed, walk in the statutes of life, without committing iniquity; he shall surely live, he shall not die.

"None of his sins that he hath committed shall be mentioned unto him: he hath done that which is lawful and right; he shall surely live.

"Yet the children of thy people say, The way of the Lord is not equal: but as for them, their way is not equal.

"When the righteous turneth from his righteousness, and committeth iniquity, he shall even die thereby.

"But if the wicked turn from his wickedness, and do that which is lawful and right, he shall live thereby." (Ezekiel 33:11-19.)

Remission of sins comes through the ordinance of baptism, and that in turn rests upon the atonement of Christ on Calvary. That sacrifice made remission of sins possible. It was that suffering that paid our debt, if we accept it; otherwise there could be no forgiveness of sins.

63

We are taught in scripture that where there is a law there is likewise a punishment attached in case of transgression. Alma explained this to his son Corianton:

"And now, the plan of mercy could not be brought about except an atonement should be made; therefore God himself atoneth for the sins of the world, to bring about the plan of mercy, to appease the demands of justice, that God might be a perfect, just God, and a merciful God also.

"Now, repentance could not come unto men except there were a punishment, which also was eternal as the life of the soul should be, affixed opposite to the plan of happiness, which was as eternal also as the life of the soul.

"Now, how could a man repent except he should sin? How could he sin if there was no law? How could there be a law save there was a punishment?

"Now, if there was no law given—if a man murdered he should die—would he be afraid he would die if he should murder?

"And also, if there was no law given against sin men would not be afraid to sin.

"And if there was no law given, if men sinned what could justice do, or mercy either, for they would have no claim upon the creature?

"But there is a law given, and a punishment affixed, and a repentance granted; which repentance mercy claimeth; otherwise, justice claimeth the creature and executeth the law, and the law inflicteth the punishment; if not so, the works of justice would be destroyed, and God would cease to be God.

"But God ceaseth not to be God, and mercy claimeth the penitent, and mercy cometh because of the atonement; and the atonement bringeth to pass the resurrection of the dead; and the resurrection of the dead bringeth back men into the presence of God; and thus they are restored into his presence, to be judged according to their works, according to the law and justice.

"For behold, justice exerciseth all his demands, and also mercy claimeth all which is her own; and thus, none but the truly penitent are saved." (Alma 42:15-24.)

The apostle John taught: "Whosoever committeth sin transgresseth also the law, for sin is the transgression of the law." (1 John 3:4.)

And the Lord told Joseph Smith: ". . . justice and judgment are the penalty which is affixed unto my law." (D&C 82:4.)

Divine mercy, however, becomes operative through the grace of Christ, who so willingly suffered for us if we would repent. As the Savior himself explained: "For behold, I, God, have suffered these things for all, that they might not suffer if they would repent." (D&C 19:16.)

Isaiah, in his remarkable predictions concerning Christ, clearly explained the vicarious suffering of the Savior in our behalf. Said he: "Surely he hath borne our griefs, and carried our sorrows. . . . he was wounded for our transgressions, he was bruised for our iniquities; . . . and with his stripes we are healed. . . . the Lord hath laid on him the iniquity of us all. . . . for the transgression of my people was he stricken. . . . he bare the sin of many, and made intercession for the transgressors." (See Isaiah 53.)

John the Baptist said to his followers as Jesus walked by: "Behold the Lamb of God, which taketh away the sin of the world." (John 1:29.)

And the apostle Peter wrote: ". . . ye know that ye were not redeemed with corruptible things, . . . But with the precious blood of Christ as of a lamb without blemish, and without spot: Who verily was foreordained before the foundation of the world." (1 Peter 1:18-20.)

Paul told the Corinthians that "Christ died for our sins according to the scriptures" (1 Corinthians 15:3), and to Timothy he declared that Christ "gave himself a ransom for all" (1 Timothy 2:6).

It is well-known that Jesus suffered so greatly in Gethsemane that he sweat drops of blood. His agony on the cross was beyond description, but there he died for us, so that if indeed we do repent and serve him, his suffering pays the penalty of our transgressions.

He gave us a sacred symbol of the crucifixion, just as he did of his burial and resurrection. It is the sacrament of the Lord's Supper. This sacred ordinance was instituted to keep ever fresh in our minds what the Lord did for us on Calvary.

As we know, the broken bread represents his torn flesh; the cup reminds us of his blood, shed in our behalf.

With great solemnity he broke bread and gave it to his disciples, both in Palestine and in ancient America. "This," he said, "shall ye do in remembrance of my body, which I have shown unto you. And it shall be a testimony unto the Father that ye do always remember me. And if ye do always remember me ye shall have my Spirit to be with you."

Then the scripture continues:

"And it came to pass that when he said these words, he commanded his disciples that they should take of the wine of the cup and drink of it, and that they should also give unto the multitude that they might drink of it.

"And it came to pass that they did so, and did drink of it and were filled; and they gave unto the multitude, and they did drink, and they were filled.

"And when the disciples had done this, Jesus said unto them: Blessed are ye for this thing which ye have done, for this is fulfilling my commandments, and this doth witness unto the Father that ye are willing to do that which I have commanded you.

"And this shall ye always do to those who repent and are baptized in my name; and ye shall do it in remembrance of my blood, which I have shed for you, that ye may witness unto the Father that ye do always remember me. And if ye do always remember me ye shall have my Spirit to be with you." (3 Nephi 18:7-11.)

The Lord gave the exact wording of the prayers to be used in the administration of the sacrament. They were given to the Nephites (Moroni 4 and 5) and presumably they were given to the Christians of the early church, since his gospel does not vary.

They were given to us by revelation through the Prophet Joseph, the first one to be used in blessing the bread, and the second, as is evident, to bless the water. (Please note that the Lord has instructed us not to use the wine of the world.)

"O God, the Eternal Father, we ask thee in the name of thy Son, Jesus Christ, to bless and sanctify this bread to the souls of all those who partake of it, that they may eat in remembrance of the body of thy Son, and witness unto thee, O God, the Eternal Father, that they are willing to take upon them the name of thy Son, and always remember him and keep his commandments which he has given them; that they may always have his Spirit to be with them. Amen.

"The manner of administering the wine—he shall take the cup also, and say:

"O God, the Eternal Father, we ask thee in the name of thy Son, Jesus Christ, to bless and sanctify this wine to the souls of all those who drink of it, that they may do it in remembrance of the blood of thy Son, which was shed for them; that they may witness unto thee, O God, the Eternal Father, that they do always remember him, that they may have his Spirit to be with them. Amen." (D&C 20:77-79.)

These prayers clearly point up the covenant we enter into as we partake of the sacramental emblems:

We eat the bread in remembrance of his broken flesh.

We drink of the cup in remembrance of his blood shed for us.

We declare that we are willing to take upon us the name of Christ.

By partaking of those emblems we declare that we will always remember him.

We covenant to keep his commandments that we may have his Spirit to be with us.

Could there be a more solemn covenant? It is sealed by our partaking of the emblems of his passion, a suffering which he said "caused myself, even God, the greatest of all, to tremble because of pain, and bleed at every pore, and suffer both body and spirit." (D&C 19:18.)

So not only do these prayers bless the sacramental emblems, but they actually place us under solemn covenants of obedience. This we must remember each week as we say "Amen" when they are said, and as we seal our pledge by eating and drinking of those emblems.

Are there any more meaningful prayers in the entire gospel? Need we not be more fully aware of their significance? Need we not obtain a deeper understanding and a better appreciation of the Lord's atonement upon which all this is based?

So these are the prayers the Lord has given us by revelation: the two sacramental prayers and the wording of the baptismal ordinance, which we generally speak of as a prayer.

The Lord invites us to pray always, in our families, over our businesses, and in all affairs, and says:

"Draw near unto me and I will draw near unto you; seek

me diligently and ye shall find me; ask, and ye shall receive; knock, and it shall be opened unto you.

"Whatsoever ye ask the Father in my name it shall be given unto you, that is expedient for you;

"And if ye ask anything that is not expedient for you, it shall turn unto your condemnation." (D&C 88:63-65.)

OUR
PRAYERS
IN PUBLIC

Elder Hartman Rector, Jr.

"And again, I command thee that thou shalt pray vocally as well as in thy heart; yea, before the world as well as in secret, in public as well as in private." (D&C 19:28.)

Public prayer, properly done, is an expression of public humility, an evidence of admission of a need or an insufficiency within the collective group assembled, an expression of reliance upon a greater power, an acknowledgment that God does in fact exist. Such a communication is an expression of belief (plus, we hope, the accompanying righteous action) and constitutes the public utterance of the combined faith of the audience.

Public prayers are offered to set a reverent tone and add solemnity to any worthwhile occasion. They are offered at the beginning and ending of state functions, religious functions, even cultural and recreational gatherings and often community or organizational meetings. They should be offered at the beginning of any great undertaking, but often are equally appropriate for even small outings. In short, prayer is proper for almost any activity engaged in by God-fearing people.

Whenever possible, one person should be designated in advance to offer the public prayer. The choice should be one who is a believer, because for prayer to be effective, there must be a consciousness of real need for prayer and real trust in God. He should be given some guidance as to the maximum time the prayer can occupy in the total program. The prayer should carefully fit within the time period allotted, and the temptation to preach a sermon while praying should be avoided. To attempt to instruct the Lord in his duties would also be out of order.

The prayer should briefly and succinctly set forth the purpose of the occasion, express thanks for blessings received, and request special blessings that are needed, using specifics and avoiding vague or well-worn phrases and generalities. It

69

should be closed in the name of Jesus Christ. The Lord's instruction in this has been constant in every age. For example, he said to Moses: "Wherefore, thou shalt do all that thou doest in the name of the Son, and thou shalt repent and call upon God in the name of the Son forevermore." (Moses 5:8.) Again in our own day the Lord gave the same instructions to Joseph Smith: "Ask the Father in my name, in faith believing that ye shall receive. . . ." (D&C 18:18.)

The language of public prayer should be respectful, using the declension of reverent pronouns, *thee* rather than the familiar *you.* In public prayers he who is voice should also speak of *we* rather than *I* because he is invoking in behalf of the whole group or audience rather than himself only. It is also well to avoid too frequent repetition of the name of God. (See D&C 107:4.)

In content the prayer should be directed to the Lord and not used to impress listeners as rhetoric. It should be neither ceremonious nor sanctimonious. Sincere, simple, direct, specific public prayer is best with appropriate consideration for the event at hand and conditions that may exist and affect all present.

Public prayer should express the gratitude, needs, desires—even fears—of the whole associated group. It is not intended to deal in personalities unless there is a particular need such as the recovery from illness of a beloved member of the group. The prayer should predominantly be an expression of thanks and a plea for help from God. We should also pray for the General Authorities of the Church, the stake and ward authorities. We should sustain them not only by voting for them and by following their instructions, but also by individual and united prayer in behalf of their physical health and strength. Also, we should pray for divine inspiration to guide them in presiding over the Church membership.

The prayer should be offered clearly in a voice that can be heard and understood by all in attendance, not in a loud voice, but neither so low that only those nearby can hear. No tone other than the normal speaking voice should be used. We do not chant or use a sing-song rhythm in prayer. It should not be hurried, but in every respect delivered in a most respectful manner that befits a petition to the Maker and Preserver of the universe.

Public occasions are great opportunities to unite our prayers for the success of the work of the Lord. "Prayer has a sanctifying effect; it unites the church; and it causes the blessings of heaven to be poured out upon the heads of the saints. We should pray for the success and triumph of all the programs of the Lord's earthly kingdom, and we should then suit our actions to our words." (Bruce R. McConkie, *Doctrinal New Testament Commentary*, Bookcraft, 1973, 3:65.)

There are a great many matters of public concern that ought to be prayed about in gatherings when the combined faith of the congregation can arise in supplication to our Father. These concerns are ever with us. We need not be engulfed with a major disaster before we can earnestly plead with the Lord. The ultimate object of all public prayers should be to bring the congregation closer to God, to be unified in the purpose to succeed in righteous endeavors. We cannot expect to have a close communion with our Heavenly Father in our daily pursuits as a people without prayer, and we should not overlook the necessity to make our prayers more efficacious by adding fasting to our preparation.

Our Heavenly Father is constant in his affirmation that he will not give without a petition from below. An Old Jewish proverb states: "Before there is a stirring above, there must be a stirring below." Then public prayer must be essential to secure the blessings of heaven or an organization. George Washington bore his testimony to this principle when he said, "No people can be bound to acknowledge and adore the Invisible Hand which conducts the affairs of men more than those of the United States. Every step by which they have advanced to the character of an independent nation seems to have been distinguished by some token of providential agency." (First Inaugural Address, 1789.)

Surely public prayer is a prerequisite to national prosperity and success. Paul indicated as much when he said, ". . . supplications, prayers, intercessions, and giving of thanks, be made for all men; For kings, and for all that are in authority; that we may lead a quiet and peaceful life in all godliness and honesty. For this is good and acceptable in the sight of God our Saviour." (1 Timothy 2:1-3.)

Abraham Lincoln surely felt as much when he said, "We have been the recipients of the choicest bounties of heaven.

We have grown in numbers, wealth and power as no other nation has ever grown, but we have forgotten God. We have become too self-sufficient to feel the necessity of redeeming
grace, too proud to pray to that God who made us. It
behooves us then to humble ourselves before the offended
power, to confess our national sins and to pray for clemency
and forgiveness." (Proclamation, April 30, 1863.)

In another part of this Proclamation he said, "It is the
duty of nations as well as of men to own their dependence
upon the over-ruling power of God, to confess their sins and
transgressions in humble sorrow; yet, with assured hope that
genuine repentance will lead to mercy and pardon and to
recognize the sublime truths announced in the Holy Scriptures and proven by all history that those nations only are
blessed whose God is the Lord. And inasmuch as we know
that by his divine law nations, like individuals, are subjected
to punishment and chastisements in this world, may we not
justly fear that the awful calamity of civil war which now
desolates the land may be but a punishment inflicted upon us
for our presumptuous sins to the needful end of our national
reformation as a whole people."

Since God seems to punish nations as well as individual
citizens for their transgressions, and since nations cannot pray,
then national repentance can come only from human leaders
and citizens. These leaders and citizens ought always to be
mindful of national problems and transgressions, and to continually beseech Almighty God through private and public
prayer in behalf of the nation.

In every nation, even while the majority of the people are
enjoying a portion of comfort, there are areas of the country
where catastrophe swells. It may be in the form of a flood, a
fire, a drought, or other death-dealing circumstances, but such
things exist constantly, and we should be aware, sympathetic,
and helpful to whatever extent is possible for us. Certainly we
have the responsibility to remain individually faithful so that
our combined prayers will be efficacious.

In times past the need for national repentance and prayer
has been pointed out by national leaders.

Benjamin Franklin stated his firm reliance on the need for
prayer among nations when he appealed for daily prayer at the
constitutional convention. The delegates had debated long

and hard with considerable bitterness when he arose and sug-
gested that clergymen be invited daily to open the session with
an invocation to God. His motion failed because there were
not sufficient funds to pay the clergy to offer prayer. I think
perhaps the Lord would have recognized prayer from the likes
of George Washington, Thomas Jefferson, and Benjamin
Franklin as quickly as he would have recogized it from an ordained clergyman.

In 1852 Daniel Webster said, "If we or our posterity reject
religious instruction and authority, violate the rules of eternal
justice, trifle with the injunctions of morality and recklessly
destroy the political constitution which holds us together, no
one can tell how sudden a catastrophe may overwhelm us that
shall bury all our glory in profound obscurity."

Today we face a similar crisis. Consider the following:

More than one million abortions were performed in the
United States in 1976.

Drug usage is at an all-time high.

An estimated 140 million people were guilty of shoplifting
in 1976.

An estimated 76 percent of employes steal from their em-
ployers.

Ten million persons in the United States are alcoholics,
with 250,000 added to the number each year. Alcohol costs
the government in lost time by employes and shoddy work-
manship an estimated $413 million annually. It is estimated
that $15 billion is made from the sale of alcohol for human
consumption in the United States each year. The grain so
used could feed 50 million starving people. One-half of all au-
tomobile accidents are alcohol-related. In addition, each
fourth death in the United States is cancer-caused. And cancer
is 15 times more prevalent among smokers than nonsmokers.

The remarks of Abraham Lincoln, Daniel Webster, and
other great patriots of the past seem to be as appropriate today
as when they were delivered more than a century ago.

It is the duty of nations as well as men to "own their dependence upon the overruling power of God, to confess their
sins and transgressions in humble sorrow." Then public
prayer becomes vital if we are to secure the blessings of heaven
to this nation.

PERSONAL
PRAYERS

Elder Marvin J. Ashton

Often as I am moved by the prayers of small children, the truth, "Except ye be converted, and become as little children, ye shall not enter into the kingdom of heaven" (Matthew 18:3), has profound significance on my mind. I am reminded that perhaps our prayers cannot enter the kingdom of God unless they are childlike in faith, humility, and purpose.

Children seem to have a very personal way of talking to God. They speak to him without fear as a friend. Yes, they seem to speak to him as if he were right there with them. Their words are powerful in directness and simplicity. Recently I listened to a young grandson begin his prayer in this manner: "Heavenly Father, thank you for Heavenly Father." Here was a four-year-old teaching powerfully and simply the lesson of appreciation for God. Children's prayers seem to get directly through because their thoughts are not filled with detours or reservations. Let me share with you one of my favorite child prayers as told years ago by the late President George Albert Smith:

"A little orphan boy was upon the operating table, ready to undergo an operation for appendicitis. . . . As the boy lay there he looked up at the surgeons—there were several of them present—and addressing the surgeon in charge he said: 'Doctor, before you begin to operate won't you pray for me?' The surgeon looked at the boy amazed and said: 'Why, I can't pray for you.' Then the little fellow turned his eyes from one to the other, asking each if they would not pray for him. Each in turn declined. Then the little man said, 'If you won't pray for me, won't you please wait while I pray for myself?' The little fellow got up on the operating table on his knees, folded his hands and uttered a prayer. He said to the Lord: 'Heavenly Father, I am only a little orphan boy but I am awful sick, and these doctors are going to operate. Will you please help them that they will do it right? And now, Heavenly Father if you will make me well I will be a good boy. Thank you for making me well.' He then turned over and laid on his back and looked up at the doctors and nurses who were all standing around, but he was the only one in the room who could see because the others had tears in their eyes. He said: 'Now I am ready.'

"A few days after that a man went into the office of the Chief Surgeon and asked him to tell him the story of the little boy he had operated on a few days before. The Surgeon said: '. . . That was the most remarkable experience of my whole life. I have operated on hundreds of men, women and children, and I have known some of them to pray, but never until I stood in the presence of that little boy, have I heard anyone talk to their Heavenly Father face to face.' " (George Albert Smith, *Sharing the Gospel with Others*, Deseret Book, 1948, pp. 144-45.)

The words of Huckleberry Finn from Mark Twain teach us another important ingredient of proper personal prayer.

"It made me shiver. And I about made up my mind to pray, and see if I couldn't try to quit being the kind of boy I was and be better. So I kneeled down. But the words wouldn't come. Why wouldn't they? It warn't no use to try and hide it from Him. . . . I knowed very well why they wouldn't come. It was because my heart warn't right; it was because . . . I was holding on to the biggest one of all. I was tryin' to make my mouth *say* I would do the right thing and the clean thing, . . . but deep down in me I knowed it was a lie, and He knowed it. You can't pray a lie—I found that out." (*The Adventures of Huckleberry Finn*, New York and Scarborough, Ontario: New American Library, 1959, pp. 208-9.)

One of the greatest blessings that can come into the life of a boy or girl is the blessing of being taught to pray while a young child. How fortunate a person is to be raised in a house of prayer. As I look back today to my youth, one of the earliest recollections I have of my parents is their helping me with my prayers before going to bed. Some of the first words I ever learned were at my mother's and father's knees when they helped me say the simple words of "Heavenly Father, bless Mommy and Daddy. Help me to be a good boy. Name of Jesus Christ. Amen." From this kind of beginning and en-couragement, it was never difficult for me to call upon my Heavenly Father to ease the pain of a bruised finger or plead for help when the family dog was run over by a car. I was taught that God was always willing to listen if I would talk to him and be good. Early, as a boy, I was taught that part of the price for having prayers answered was good conduct. Many times when my boyhood prayers were not answered as immediately as I thought they should be I never turned my back on God; instead, I lectured myself for not being worthy or in tune.

I vividly recall as a young boy holding "graveside services" for my poisoned dog Blackie. When he died despite my tearful prayers, a couple of my buddies joined me in conducting a funeral. I don't think we did much preaching that day, but I do recall there was a lot of praying. Today I look back with gratitude that I lived in a home and neighborhood where parents and older friends and neighbors didn't make fun when we asked God to take care of our friend who had now gone to live with him in heaven.

From these beginnings I learned early that personal prayers are our own business, and nothing is too unimportant for God. A number of times just before my mother passed away, she seemed to delight in telling my wife in front of me that when as a young boy I learned to say my prayers by myself, I refused help because I wanted to say "my own."

With this kind of background, I suppose it won't be too difficult for the reader to understand my attitude regarding prayer when I share an experience of a number of months ago. I was traveling by airplane between Salt Lake City and Chicago. The flight was routine and uneventful until we were about one hundred miles out of Chicago. At this point we encountered a severe storm with the turbulence becoming extreme. The pilot instructed us to fasten our seat belts tightly and remain in our seats for the remainder of the flight. As we circled Chicago awaiting our turn for landing, some of the air bumps were breathtaking and abrupt. The bad weather had caused delay in our approach turn, and as we became uncomfortable in our bumpy holding pattern, some passengers became nervous as well as anxious. One lady in the plane about two rows back of me who recognized me said in a loud but trembling voice, "Elder Ashton, don't you think we had better pray?" I turned my head, looked back at her, and replied, "I said my prayers this morning." When we were safely on the ground, I was pleased to learn this lady, whom I did not know, was not offended, but rather thanked me for teaching her a lesson.

To be effective, prayers must not consist of words alone. Earnest prayers must have an appropriate blend of earnest feeling and spirit. It is the spirit that not only teaches a man to pray, but also makes his heartfelt desires acceptable and conveyable. If a contrite spirit and a broken heart are united with faith unwavering, our prayers, no matter how simple the words, will be significant.

"And now, my beloved brethren, I perceive that ye ponder still in your hearts; and it grieveth me that I must speak concerning this thing. For if ye would hearken unto the Spirit which teacheth a man to pray ye would know that ye must pray; for the evil spirit teacheth not a man to pray, but teacheth him that he must not pray.

"But behold, I say unto you that ye must pray always, and not faint; that ye must not perform any thing unto the Lord save in the first place ye shall pray unto the Father in the name of Christ, that he will consecrate thy performance unto thee, that thy performance may be for the welfare of thy soul." (2 Nephi 32:8-9.)

Our personal prayers need not be long, but I think it appropriate to remind all that they should be more frequent. We do need to thank God in all things and ask for his help in our keeping all of his commandments. We have been commanded to pray under all conditions wherever we are. Our spirits are heaven-drawn, anxious for constant communication with the source of all great strength. The Savior set a beautiful pattern as shared in 3 Nephi 19:17-34:

"And it came to pass that when they had all knelt down upon the earth, he commanded his disciples that they should pray.

"And behold, they began to pray; and they did pray unto Jesus, calling him their Lord and their God.

"And it came to pass that Jesus departed out of the midst of them, and went a little way off from them and bowed himself to the earth, and he said:

"Father, I thank thee that thou hast given the Holy Ghost unto these whom I have chosen; and it is because of their belief in me that I have chosen them out of the world.

"Father, I pray thee that thou wilt give the Holy Ghost unto all them that shall believe in their words.

"Father, thou hast given them the Holy Ghost because they believe in me; and thou seest that they believe in me because thou hearest them, and they pray unto me; and they pray unto me because I am with them.

"And now Father, I pray unto thee for them, and also for all those who shall believe on their words, that they may believe in me, that I may be in them as thou, Father, art in me, that we may be one.

"And it came to pass that when Jesus had thus prayed unto the Father, he came unto his disciples, and behold, they did still continue, without ceasing, to pray unto him; and they did not multiply many words, for it was given unto them what they should pray, and they were filled with desire.

"And it came to pass that Jesus blessed them as they did pray unto him; and his countenance did smile upon them, and the light of his countenance did shine upon them, and behold they were as white as the countenance and also the garments of Jesus; and behold the whiteness thereof did exceed all the whiteness, yea, even there could be nothing upon earth so white as the whiteness thereof.

"And Jesus said unto them: Pray on; nevertheless they did not cease to pray.

"And he turned from them again, and went a little way off and bowed himself to the earth; and he prayed again unto the Father, saying:

"Father, I thank thee that thou hast purified those whom I have chosen, because of their faith, and I pray for them, and also for them who shall believe on their words, that they may be purified in me, through faith on their words, even as they are purified in me.

"Father, I pray not for the world, but for those whom thou has given me out of the world, because of their faith, that they may be purified in me, that I may be in them as thou, Father, art in me, that we may be one, that I may be glorified in them.

"And when Jesus had spoken these words he came again unto his disciples; and behold they did pray steadfastly, without ceasing, unto him; and he did smile upon them again; and behold they were white, even as Jesus.

"And it came to pass that he went again a little way off and prayed unto the Father;

"And tongue cannot speak the words which he prayed, neither can be written by man the words which he prayed.

"And the multitude did hear and do bear record; and their hearts were open and they did understand in their hearts the words which he prayed.

"Nevertheless, so great and marvelous were the words which he prayed, that they cannot be written, neither can they be uttered by man."

The Savior would say to all "Pray on, pray on." Daily dependence upon God through prayer brings strength, growth, and personal stature. I have tried to teach my sons and daughters to pray constantly because I know of prayer's power and soul-satisfying refreshment. I know God hears and answers prayers. He has heard and answered mine on many occasions. As a couple, my wife and I have learned to pray individually in private and in secret that our prayers might be answered in a similar setting. We have tried to make our personal prayers simple and honest, trying always to include in our pleadings, "Father, thy will be done," and leave the manner, time, and nature of our blessings to him in his ultimate wisdom. We need to make our personal prayers sincere and void of vain repetitions.

"And when thou prayest, thou shalt not be as the hypocrites are: for they love to pray standing in the synagogues and in the corners of the streets, that they may be seen of men. Verily I say unto you, they have their reward.

"But thou, when thou prayest, enter into thy closet, and when thou hast shut thy door, pray to thy Father which is in secret; and thy Father which seeth in secret shall reward thee openly.

"But when ye pray, use not vain repetitions, as the heathen do: for they think that they shall be heard for their much speaking.

"Be not ye therefore like unto them: for your Father knoweth what things ye have need of, before ye ask him.

"After this manner therefore pray ye: Our Father which art in heaven, Hallowed be thy name.

"Thy kingdom come, Thy will be done in earth, as it is in heaven.

"Give us this day our daily bread.

"And forgive us our debts, as we forgive our debtors.

"And lead us not into temptation, but deliver us from evil; for thine is the kingdom, and the power, and the glory, for ever. Amen." (Matthew 6:5-13.)

For more than twenty years I had the opportunity of directing and supervising M Men basketball in the Church. Before I had this responsibility, I played a lot of basketball, and I will always be grateful for the lessons I learned on and off of the court. I don't think I ever played on a team, including the ones I played on while serving as a missionary in England, that didn't unite in prayer before a game. In addition to these prayers, I always found it helpful and rewarding to have my own private prayers before the team prayer. Often these personal prayers were silent reflections while putting on my basketball uniform. On many occasions while supervising MIA athletics, I encouraged teams and players to pray after the game as well as before. I believe some did, but not very many. I recall trying to discipline myself to pray after a game, especially after a bitter defeat. I made it a few times, but as I look back, the occasions were infrequent. Following some of those defeats, I recall rationalizing myself into thinking it wouldn't be honest to give a prayer of thanks when "We were robbed from victory by a lousy referee or a poorer team that just happened to 'luck out' in the final seconds."

"A Father's Prayer" by General Douglas MacArthur has always been a favorite writing of mine. I never tire of its simplicity and depth.

"Build me a son, O Lord, who will be strong enough to know when he is weak, and brave enough to face himself when he's afraid; one who will be proud of unbending in honest defeat, and humble and gentle in victory.

"Build me a son whose wishbone will not be where his backbone should be; a son who will know Thee—and that to know himself is the foundation stone of knowledge.

"Lead him, I pray, not in the path of ease and comfort, but under the stress and spur of difficulties and challenge. Here let him learn to stand up in the storm; here let him learn compassion for those who fail.

"Build me a son whose heart will be clear, whose goal will be high; a son who will master himself before he seeks to master other men; one who will learn to laugh, yet never forget how to weep; one who will reach into the future, yet never forget the past.

"After all these things are his, add, I pray, enough of a sense of humor, so that he may not always be serious, yet never take himself too seriously. Give him humility, so that he may always remember the simplicity of true greatness, the open mind of true wisdom, the meekness of true strength.

"Then, I, his father, will dare to whisper, 'I have not lived in vain.' " (Robert B. Fox, *Pray Without Ceasing*, Deseret Book, 1961, p. 12.)

In counseling with couples about to marry or those already married, I always suggest daily prayers. There is a peculiar daily strength and power that comes to a couple united in prayerful communication to God. I suggest that the marriage partners take turns being voice for each in crying out words of appreciation and dependence. God will help the couple who sincerely and worthily invite him into their family circle and personal lives. On a one-to-one basis or as a couple, God will be as close to us as we will have him. All couples as well as families and individuals need to remind themselves that putting themselves into a proper attitude to appropriately pray often supplies the necessary oil for the troubled waters of the day. Personal prayer is not only power, it is preparation.

All of our thoughts should be heaven oriented. Victor Hugo once said, "Certain thoughts are prayers. There are moments when, whatever be the attitude of the body, the soul is on its knees." Certainly every soul has a sincere desire to pray. Personal prayer is a sign of strength. Personal prayer is a sign of dependency. Personal prayer is an acknowledgment of someone greater whose power and guidance are needed.

Early in my missionary service in England while tracting one day, I was told by a man that his next-door neighbor was a member of the Reorganized Church of Jesus Christ, and that he was just waiting to have Mormon missionaries knock at his door.

The neighbor was represented as being bitter toward our church and anxious to belittle and embarrass at the first opportunity. My contact invited me to "take on" his neighbor, and then politely closed his own door. As I stood there, only two months in the mission field and a senior companion, I wondered if my companion and I were ready for this type of confrontation.

While I was trying to decide whether we should avoid what could become an unpleasant situation or go about our business, I offered a silent prayer for help. In my heart I knew I was going to knock on that door, so I prayed for our ability with God's help to make a friend. We knocked on the door, were invited in, and sat with this couple. Immediately it was evident we had been invited in so the man could work us over in the privacy of his own home. We listened courteously under trying circumstances. I felt the Lord helping us to avoid verbal retaliation. When we were allowed speaking time, I recall that the only thing we shared was our testimonies. The visit ended with our friends buying a copy of the *Millennial Star* and inviting us back for another visit. As we left that house and walked down the street, I will never forget the personal satisfaction resulting from the prayers of two elders with combined missionary experience of less than three months.

Personal prayers can be offered in many ways. Whether we commune vocally, in private, in song, or in meditation, God can and does respond. Who is to say prayers of "lead me, guide me, walk beside me, help me find the way" are not most acceptable, whether they fall from the lips of children or humble adults. He is available to us day or night and under all circumstances; to this I bear my testimony.

"Counsel with the Lord in all thy doings, and he will direct thee for good; yea, when thou liest down at night lie down unto the Lord, that he may watch over you in your sleep; and when thou risest in the morning let thy heart be full of thanks unto God; and if ye do these things, ye shall be lifted up at the last day." (Alma 37:37.)

We need to constantly prepare ourselves to do the will of our Father. He will hear us and give us entrance into his kingdom according to our personal performances. Our prayers will not be heard if we worship and plead with our lips only. The personal prayers of the righteous and sincerely repentant are a joy to our Father.

"Not every one that saith unto me, Lord, Lord, shall enter into the kingdom of heaven; but he that doeth the will of my Father which is in heaven.

"Many will say to me in that day, Lord, Lord, have we not

prophesied in thy name? and in thy name have cast out devils? and in thy name done many wonderful works?

"And then will I profess unto them, I never knew you: depart from me, ye that work iniquity." (Matthew 7:21-23.)

Brigham Young once said, "Prayer keeps a man from sin, and sin keeps a man from prayer."

Let us so live that our contrite spirits and humble hearts will make it possible for us to continually communicate with God. Sin can and does keep mankind from prayer. I pray our Heavenly Father will help us to make our personal prayers childlike and continuing as we endeavor to walk uprightly in his strength.

FAMILY PRAYER

President Spencer W. Kimball

A prominent writer and marriage counselor has written: ". . . strong family life is indispensable, not merely to the culture but actually the survival of any people. In the history of mankind one nation after another has followed this pattern [of degrading family life and substituting other patterns for it] and they had disappeared. . . . For the well being of the community; for the very existence of the nation, one of the first questions asked about any proposed change in the culture should be, 'Will it strengthen the family?' " (Dr. Paul Popenoe, *Family Life*, September 1972.)

The Lord organized the whole program in the beginning, with a father who procreates, provides, and loves and directs, and a mother who conceives and bears and nurtures and feeds and trains. The Lord could have organized it otherwise, but he chose to have a unit with responsibility and purposeful associations where children train and discipline each other and come to love, honor, and appreciate each other. The family is the great plan of life as conceived and organized by our Father in heaven.

To any thoughtful person it must be obvious that intimate association without marriage is sin; that children without parenthood and family life is tragedy; that society without basic family life is without foundation and will disintegrate into nothingness and oblivion.

The Father knew all this when he gave this command to his children in November 1831. He was not arguing that there should be families. He seemed to take that for granted, and commanded: "Inasmuch as parents have children in Zion, . . . they shall also teach their children to pray and to walk uprightly before the Lord." (D&C 68:25, 28.)

Once when I talked to leaders in a foreign country where different ideologies touch their children, I asked how the parents were able to hold their children and keep them from evil. Their reply was so natural and so proper:

"We train our children in our homes so completely in the way of right and truth that the destructive, godless philosophies and heresies of their other teachers run off without penetrating, like water on a duck's back, and our children remain true to the faith."

Ah, that is the answer. Family life, home life, home evenings, dedicated, selfless parents. That is the way the Lord ordained our lives to be.

More than a decade ago a major in the U.S. Air Force told of his test flights. He was born of goodly parents who taught him righteousness. He had flown 25 different types of military aircraft in 4,000 hours in the air. He had flown 142 combat missions and had received many distinguished medals. He told us that "before takeoff every pilot takes a few moments to make a last-minute check of his engine, flight controls, hydraulic and pneumatic systems and other essential subsystems of his aircraft to be sure the flight can at least begin safely. . . . His reactions to emergency conditions must be as instinctive and as infallible as human thought and reflexes permit.

". . . Yet, there is something missing on the printed checklist which to me has become as necessary to a successful flight as lowering the wheels for a smooth landing. It is a prayer to ask my Father in heaven to bless me that my best judgment and skill will guide my actions, especially in periods of stress. There have been several instances . . . in which I know the answer to this prayer has been received with dramatic suddenness."

Being born of goodly parents in a goodly home with goodly training in his infancy, childhood, and youth, he seemed to feel secure in his hazardous work. He was unafraid, for he was prepared. He knew the power of the Lord's statement: "If ye are prepared, ye shall not fear." (D&C 38:30.)

That preparation comes from infancy and childhood training, when faith is born and character established. If children are tuned in on the right wave length, if they are taught early the responsibilities of time and eternities, they will usually react properly when engulfed in emergencies. If they have consciously and faithfully done all that is expected of them, nothing can be too far wrong. The Nephite prophet insisted: ". . . ye must pour out your souls in your closets, and your secret places; and in your wilderness." (Alma 34:26.)

And what a great legacy to our children Isaiah promised: "And all thy children shall be taught of the Lord; and great shall be the peace of thy children." (Isaiah 54:13.)

Surely every good parent would like this peace for his offspring. It comes from the simple life of the true Latter-day Saint as he makes his home and family supreme.

"Pray in your families unto the Father, always in my name, that your wives and your children may be blessed." (3 Nephi 18:21.)

Is that too much to ask?

I was once in Idaho Falls, Idaho, as a guest in the home of a typical Latter-day Saint family. There was a dedicated set of parents and many children. The oldest was in military service in the South Pacific, and the hearts of the family followed him from place to place. They handed me his latest letter from the war zone. This is what I read:

"There have been times when we were so scared, we would tremble, but the fear was out of our minds with prayer and the knowledge that we were being guided by the Lord. Dad, I love my religion and I am proud that I had someone like you and Mother to teach me to pray. Then I also know that you are praying for me each morning and night."

Spirituality is born in the home and is nurtured in home evenings, in twice-a-day and oftener daily prayers, in weekly meetings when the family goes to church together. That spirituality as the foundation of one's life comes to his rescue when emergency strikes.

Security is not born of inexhaustible wealth, but of unquenchable faith. And generally that kind of faith is born and nurtured in the home and in childhood.

From World War II comes a story of a young Utah boy who was called to serve his country in the faraway places across several time zones. On his wrist he wore the conventional wristband watch to tell him the time in the area in which he was living. But strangely enough he carried a larger, heavier old-time watch in his pocket, which gave another time of day. His buddies noted that frequently he would look at his wrist watch, then turn to the old-fashioned one in his pocket, and this led them, in their curiosity, to ask him why the additional watch. Unembarrassed, he promptly said:

"The wrist watch tells me the time here where we are, but the big watch which Pa gave me tells me that time it is in Utah. You see," he continued, "mine is a large family—a very close family. When the big watch says 5 a.m. I know Dad is rolling out to milk the cows. And any night when it says 7:30, I know the whole family is around a well-spread table on their knees thanking the Lord for what's on the table and asking Him to watch over me and keep me clean and honorable. It's those things that make me want to fight when the goin' gets tough. . . . I can find out what time it is here easy enough. What I want to know is what time it is in *Utah.*" (Adapted from Vaughn R. Kimball, "The Right Time at Home," *Reader's Digest,* May 1944, p. 43.)

I knew this family well. I knew this sailor slightly. I knew this father. His cows had to feed a large family, but his greater interest was the growing children who needed more than milk and bread. I have knelt in mighty prayer with this wonderful family. The home training has carried through to the eternal blessing of this large family.

O my beloved brothers and sisters, what a world it would be if the members of every family in this church were to be on their knees like this every night and morning! And what a world it would be if hundreds of millions of families in this great land and other lands were praying for their sons and daughters twice daily. And what a world this would be if a billion families throughout the world were in home evenings and church activity and were on their physical knees pouring out their souls for their children, their families, their leaders, their governments!

This kind of family could bring us back toward the translation experience of righteous Enoch. The millennium would be ushered in. Enoch was asked questions about himself. He answered, among other things, ". . . my father taught me in all the ways of God." (Moses 6:41.) And Enoch walked with God and he was *not,* for God took him.

Enoch and his people dwelt in righteousness in the city of Holiness, even Zion. And Zion was taken up into heaven.

Yes, here is the answer: righteous, teaching parents; obedient, loving children; faithfulness to family duties. These qualities in a home make for security and character in the lives of children.

TEACHING
OUR CHILDREN
TO PRAY

Elder Vaughn J. Featherstone

The family unit is truly the most important organization in time or eternity. President David O. McKay said, "No other success in life can compensate for failure in the home." President Harold B. Lee declared, "The greatest work we will ever do is the work we do within the walls of our own home."

I believe that every young person has a basic belief in prayer. As parents we, by our example, need to teach our children how to pray, to provide lifelong stability and security for them. Children who see other members of the family go to the Lord in prayer learn to rely on communion with Heavenly Father when they themselves are in need.

I did not grow up in a home where we were taught to pray nor where we had family prayer. My father, though he was a member of the Church, was inactive, and my mother joined the Church when we children were older. As a young boy of eight or nine I recall being invited to attend Primary. I well remember the lessons on prayer. I did not know how to pray, so I memorized the Lord's Prayer. Sometimes I felt as if I needed to say it several times before I got through to Heavenly Father. What a blessing it would have been if I had been taught how to pray properly! How I wish I had been taught the four simple parts to prayer, which our Primary teachers today teach:

1. We address our Father in heaven.
2. We express our gratitude and love for him.
3. We ask for special blessings.
4. We close our prayers in the name of Jesus Christ.

Such prayers, simple and sweet, are heard. As we grow older, we never come to the end of growth in our ability of pray. Changing conditions in our health, work, personal welfare, perplexities, frustrations, discouragements, and needs increase the intensity of our prayers. What a sweet experience for young children or teenagers to join with us in our family prayers! What a blessing it is for them to know that their private, individual prayers are heard and answered by a kind, wise, loving Heavenly Father, and that they can take their problems—no matter how simplistic they may be—to him in prayer!

My wife and I have seven children, six sons and a daughter. Each one of our children has been taught to pray as soon as he or she was old enough to kneel. Some of the sweetest prayers ever offered in our home have been those of our children. Many times we as adults forget how teachable children are, and how much they can learn if we give them guidance and encouragement. Sometimes parents are overly permissive or too lax in their teaching, thinking their children do not comprehend. They comprehend more than we would suppose. They can be taught to pray at a very early age.

My wife, Merlene, has knelt with our little ones in prayer and has taught them specific things to say, concepts that will be a strength to them all their lives. For example, our son Paul, who is just two and a half, has been saying little prayers for nearly a year now. He has been kneeling since he was about nine or ten months old. (Of course someone had to hold him.)

We always pray for other members of the family. Each prayer also includes these words: "Heavenly Father, help us to be prepared and worthy to go on missions. Help us to be pure and worthy to be married in the temple." Merlene is teaching Paul to always include the words, "Heavenly Father, I love thee and I know that thou dost love me." What a marvelous strength those words will be in times of testing or trial!

Heavenly Father is accessible to us all, both young and old. In my own life there have been moments when I have felt an overwhelming, absolute need for intervention by a kind Father in heaven. Our children learn great trust in prayer as we share with them these personal experiences.

When our fifth son, Lawrence, was born, my wife had complications in labor, and the doctor stayed by her side all day. She also had had a dream that frightened her. She dreamed that two men in black clothes had come to get her, and she feared this may have been a warning she might not make it through the delivery. Late that night the doctor asked me to leave the room so he could examine her again. Greatly concerned about her, I went out into the hall, stood by a window looking over the twinkling lights of the Salt Lake Valley, and, with tears in my eyes, pleaded with the Lord to spare her life.

While I was praying, someone came rushing down the hallway. I saw a nurse run into my wife's room, then come out, get a cart with a tank of oxygen, and wheel the cart into the room. Now I knew my wife was in great danger. Although I thought I had been praying with all my heart, I suddenly found I could pray with even greater humility and pleading. I promised the Lord I would do anything I was ever asked to do in the Church if he would spare Merlene's life. The prayer was offered with every particle of my being.

In a few moments the door opened, and they were wheeling her to the delivery room. Lawrence, weighing ten pounds and twelve ounces, was born shortly after, and his mother soon recovered her health. Our prayers had been answered.

When Lawrence was thirteen we were expecting our seventh child, and again I was concerned for my wife's well-being. I tried not to alarm my family. However, I had told Lawrence about some of the difficulties connected with his birth, and this affected him greatly.

When I took Merlene to the hospital I told the family I would call them and let them know how their mother was and whether they had a little brother or sister. After Paul was born, I called home and Lawrence answered. I told him the good news and said I would be home in a little while. When I went home I told them all about their new baby brother and that their mother was doing well. That evening as I left the house to go to the hospital, Lawrence handed me a letter to give to his mother. When I arrived, I gave her a kiss, then handed her the letter. Her eyes moistened as she read it; then she handed it to me. It said:

"To my favorite and most loved Mother. Congratulations. When Dad phoned us and told us we had a little brother I just about freaked. After you left to go to the hospital I went in Dad's den and knelt down to have prayer to ask Heavenly Father to bless you that you would be all right. Well my prayer was answered. After Dad came home he told how just before the baby was born you gritted your teeth and tears flowed down your cheeks but you wouldn't cry out. I kind of

got this unstuckable lump in my throat.
"I'm working on my hiking merit badge.
Love, Lawrence"

Faith is often more pure in our children than it is in us. As adults, we tend to justify our lack of faith with our sense of practicality. Oftentimes we unthinkingly raise questions and doubts that lead them to modify their faith to our level of lesser faith. But children have a sweet, unquestioning trust in Heavenly Father, and we need to help them nurture this simple faith.

When our second son, Dave, was twelve years old, he was home alone one afternoon when the telephone rang. It was one of the Laurels in our ward who was calling. Her car had a flat tire and she had been unable to find anyone to help her fix it, so she called to see if my wife, who was president of the Young Women of the ward, could help her. Dave said, "I'm home alone, but I can ride my bike and help you change the tire." When he hung up the phone, he remembered he hadn't asked her where she was. He went into his bedroom, knelt down, and asked the Lord to take him to this girl. Then he went out, climbed on his bicycle, and rode directly to where she was.

In my own life I recall an experience in my boyhood that made a lasting impression on me. May I share it with you.

When I was a deacon in the Aaronic Priesthood, the member of the bishopric who advised the deacons quorum came into our quorum meeting the Sunday before Thanksgiving and said, "I hope we won't have one member of this quorum who won't kneel down in family prayer and have a blessing on the food this Thanksgiving." It was 1943, and our country was engaged in World War II. We discussed our need for a divine blessing for those who were in military service and for all the other difficulties we as a nation were facing. We also talked about the blessings we each enjoyed. Then we were again encouraged to have family prayer.

A heavy cloud settled on my heart. I didn't know how our family could have family prayer. My father had a drinking problem, and my mother was not a member of the Church at that time. We had never had a prayer in our home, not even a blessing on the food. After quorum meeting I continued to consider the challenge, and finally concluded we would not be able to have prayer.

That evening at sacrament meeting the bishop stood up at the close of the meeting and said, "Brothers and sisters, Thursday is Thanksgiving. I hope we will not have one family in the ward that will not kneel in family prayer. We ought to express our gratitude for the great goodness of our Heavenly Father to us." And then he enumerated some of our many blessings.

Again it seemed as if my soul was filled with an ominous gloom. I tried to figure out a way our family could have prayer. I thought about it Monday, and again on Tuesday, and on Wednesday. On Wednesday evening my father did not return home from work at the normal hour, and I knew from experience that, because it was payday, he was satisfying his thirst for alcohol. When he finally came at two in the morning quite an argument ensued. I lay in bed wondering how we could ever have prayer with that kind of contention in our home.

On Thanksgiving morning, we did not eat breakfast so we could eat more dinner. My four brothers and I went out to play with some neighbor boys. We decided to dig a hole and make a trench to it and cover it over as a clubhouse. We dug a deep hole, and with every shovelful of dirt I threw out of the hole I thought about family prayer for Thanksgiving. I wondered if I would have enough courage to suggest to my parents that we have a prayer, but I was afraid I would not. I wondered if my older brother, who has always been an ideal in my life, would suggest it, since he had been in the same sacrament meeting and had heard the bishop's suggestion.

Finally, at about 2:30 in the afternoon, Mother told us to come get cleaned up for dinner. Then we sat down at the big round oak table. Dad sat down with us silently—he and Mother were not speaking to each other. As she brought in the platter with the beautiful golden brown turkey, my young heart was about to burst. I thought, *Now please, won't someone suggest we have a family prayer?* I thought the words over and over, but they wouldn't come out. I turned and looked at my older brother, praying desperately that he would suggest prayer. The bowls of delicious food were being passed around the table; plates were being filled; and time and opportunity were passing. I knew that if someone did not act immediately, it would be too late. Then suddenly, as always, everyone just started eating.

My heart sank, and despair filled my soul. Although I had worked up a great appetite, and Mother was a marvelous cook, I wasn't hungry. I just wanted to pray.

I resolved that day that no son or daughter of mine would ever want to pray and not be able to do it because of shyness or lack of courage. In our family we have family prayers, personal prayers, and blessings on every meal. As one who has known the contrast between families that do not pray and those that do, I know the value of prayer in the home and in the life of every child and youth in the Church.

It is good to share with our children faith-promoting stories that teach them how to respond to answers to prayer and listen to the promptings of the Spirit. One such story is the one President Harold B. Lee told, of how as a young boy he decided he would go to a neighbor's property to explore an old building. As he climbed through the fence he heard a voice telling him not to go over there. He obediently responded and did not continue on. Because of his obedience he may never know what the price of disobedience would have been. We need to teach our children that it is better not to find out than to experience the consequences of disobedience. Satan uses curiosity in us all to tempt us and lead us in his directions. There are some things we don't need to know. President Lee did not need to know why he should stay away from the old building.

Some time ago a couple came to my office with very heavy hearts. They had a son who was of priest age, an Eagle Scout, a Duty-to-God award winner, a good student who had been conscientious in school and on his part-time job. Then one night he just walked away from home and didn't return. He had been gone for several weeks, and they were heartsick.

I asked them if they had pleaded with the Lord to know where their son was. They assured me they had. "Have you pleaded with all your strength?" "Yes, we have." "Have you pleaded with every particle of your being?" "Well," they said, "maybe not every particle." I said, "You go home and pray again—this time with every particle of energy and strength of your being." They said they would.

That afternoon the couple knelt down at about three o'clock, and they spent one hour on their knees, pleading with the Lord. At six o'clock the phone rang. It was their son, calling from Banff, Alberta, Canada. After talking to him for a few minutes and finding that he was safe and in no danger, they asked why he had called at that particular time. He replied, "The bishop this evening had the strongest impression to have me call home. He came over to my apartment and said he would not leave until I called home."

We need to teach our children that some things demand pleading with the Lord. When we come to know that without his help we cannot possibly accomplish our desires, then we must learn to plead to whatever extent necessary.

As parents, we teach our children "to walk in the light" when we teach them to pray. Great blessings are wrought through prayer. The God of heaven would not expect us to pray to him if he had no intention of answering our prayers.

One of the choicest experiences of my life was to kneel in prayer with a mature couple in the office of President Spencer W. Kimball. I felt President Kimball's overpowering love for our Father in heaven as we knelt together. He taught us much about prayer through his example. We as parents ever and always will teach more by our example than by precept.

In summary, then, let me suggest that we need to teach our children to pray at the earliest possible age. They need to be taught to believe that answers to prayers truly are forthcoming. They need to see a life-long example of parents who know how to pray. They need to understand that sometimes it takes pleading with the Lord to humble us to the dust of the earth before answers come. They need to learn that we should pray as though everything depended upon God, and then work as though everything depended upon us. When we follow through on our part of the agreement with our Heavenly Father, answers always come. And as parents, we can learn from our children the power that is found in simple, pure, unquestioning faith. May the Lord bless us as parents in fulfilling these sacred responsibilities.

FAITH
AND PRAYER

Elder Joseph Anderson

It has been truly said that the greatest asset of a man or a nation is faith, that the men who built this country and made it prosper during its darkest days were men with unshakable faith, men of courage, men of vision, men who always looked forward and never backward.

The same can be said in truth of those who established this church under the inspiration and revelation of the Lord and of those who have built upon the foundation they laid. They too were and are men of unfailing testimony and unwavering faith.

I think perhaps there has never been greater need for faith than is the need today, particularly faith in divine leadership. Members of The Church of Jesus Christ of Latter-day Saints, as a general rule, have faith in divine leadership, but the world needs faith in God, that he rules the world; and the people of this nation and the world need that faith, faith in the God of this land and faith in the God of the world, who is Jesus Christ.

Many of us have had the experience of being on a ship traveling on the ocean. As we look in the various directions, we can see nothing but water. As far as the mortal eye can see, the sky comes down and meets the water. The sun comes up on the horizon, and in the evening the sun sets on the horizon. The same is true when we are on the ground; the limit of our vision is the horizon. Is it not true also that the limit of our spiritual perception is the horizon we see?

What about our spiritual horizon? Is it limited to our present struggle for the things of this world? Is it limited to an acquisition of things of the flesh? Is our horizon limited to our competition with a money-mad world, to the obtaining of the worldly things of life, or does it reach out to an eternity with God and our loved ones in the life to come?

Our horizon should extend to an unlimited future beyond death—out beyond those things of a temporal nature. Our horizon of the future should not be confused with the close-up horizon of present conditions.

Our philosophy of life contemplates an eternity of life—life without beginning before we came here, life without end hereafter. Our happiness here and hereafter depends upon our actions here. We should therefore seek the finer things of life. The road leading to eternal life must be paved with obedience to the commandments of the Lord.

We once dwelt in the presence of our Father, in the spirit, and we rejoiced at the opportunity to come to earth and take upon ourselves mortality and pass through the experiences we here encounter, that we might prove ourselves worthy of greater experiences and greater blessings.

While here we are not to enjoy the presence of our Father, but we can communicate with him, and we can hear his voice if that becomes necessary. The Holy Ghost is given to us as our guide and companion and monitor, if we live worthy of that blessing.

It seems difficult for some to have faith in an eternal being and that he can communicate with man; that he hears and answers our prayers; that he is the Father of our spirits, for we are dual beings, spiritual and physical; that he loves us; that he has given us commandments which, if we accept and live them, will result in mortal as well as eternal blessings to us.

There was a time when men would have laughed to scorn anyone who would have said that in time to come we would be able to sit in our homes and watch and see and hear by means of television and radio things that are transpiring today in our own country, in Europe or Asia, South America or Africa.

In our time we have seen men walk on the moon; we have heard the messages they have sent over the great expanse of space between us and the moon; and we have witnessed pictures they were transmitting.

These things have been accomplished by faith, by work, and by intelligence.

Can we talk with God?

Can our prayers, even in thought as well as word, ascend to the Father of us all, and does he have the power to make answer thereto?

We lived by sight in the spirit state before we came here;

we are walking by faith in this mortal existence. The Spirit of God bears witness to the spirit of man that we are God's children; that he loves us; and that there is a purpose to earth life, a great and mighty purpose, a glorious purpose; that by keeping the commandments that he has given us we may gain knowledge and understanding; that we may gain experience by overcoming the opposition with which we must contend; that we shall resurrect from the grave in the due time of the Lord and eventually return into his presence if we live worthily. This is the long-distance horizon we should keep in view.

Alma, a Book of Mormon prophet, relates an experience in his time about a people who were cast out of the synagogues because of the coarseness of their apparel, a people who were poor as to the things of this world and were also poor in heart. They came unto Alma, explaining their situation, and asked what they should do. Alma answered by explaining to them the principle of faith and teaching them the word of God.

Concerning faith he states that "faith is not to have a perfect knowledge of things; therefore if ye have faith ye hope for things which are not seen, which are true." (Alma 32:21.)

Alma then goes on to compare his words, which are truly the word of God and the gospel of salvation, to a seed that a man plants in the soil. He suggests that if we will give place that a seed may be planted in our hearts, and not cast it out or resist the Spirit of the Lord, if it is a true seed it will swell within the breast; and when one feels this swelling motion he cannot do otherwise than admit that the seed is a good seed, for it enlargeth the soul and beginneth to enlighten one's understanding, and it becomes delicious to the individual. Further, when the seed, or the word, or the gospel, swells and sprouts and begins to grow in your soul, you know it is a good seed, and therefore your knowledge is perfect; it is no longer faith but knowledge.

People sometimes say that one cannot know that the gospel is true. As indicated by Alma, if, when you hear the word of God, you do not cast it out by unbelief or resist the Spirit of the Lord, the swellings within your breast, its enlargement of your soul, and its enlightening of your understanding are of such a nature that they cause you to know that it is the truth.

However, this is only a beginning. You must nourish the seed; in other words, you must nourish the testimony that you have that it is true, by living the teachings of the gospel.

If you will do this, this ancient prophet tells us, the seed will grow into a tree and bring forth fruit. But if the tree is neglected, it will not take root; and when the heat of the sun cometh and scorcheth it, it will wither and die. This is not because the seed or the word of God was not true nor because the fruit thereof would not be desirable, but it is because the ground was barren and the plant or the tree was not nourished, in which event one cannot have the fruit thereof that he otherwise would obtain.

If, however, you have faith and patience to nourish the word, or the tree, as time goes on you may pluck the fruit thereof, which is most precious and delicious to the taste.

I testify to you that if you do these things—truly try this experiment regarding the word of God as contained in the gospel of Jesus Christ and live in accordance with the commandments therein set forth, nourishing the truths of the gospel—you shall have the privilege of feasting upon this fruit; your faith will be fully rewarded and will develop into a sure knowledge of the truth of the gospel of Jesus Christ.

We testify that when occasion requires, the voice of God can be heard by the Lord's latter-day prophets; that they can tune in through the instrument of faith; and that even you and I can see beyond the veil, if it is in accordance with the Lord's will and if we are in tune with the Infinite.

The Latter-day Saints believe and teach that without the experience of mortal life, its problems and accomplishments, and without a resurrected body, the spirit of man cannot have a fullness of joy. Our philosophy of life contemplates an eternity of existence—life without beginning in the preexistent world and life hereafter throughout the eternities.

Our happiness in this life and in the life to come depends upon our actions here. If we are to attain the goal of eternal salvation and exaltation in the kingdom of our Heavenly Father, we must hold fast to the iron rod, which is the word of God, and render obedience to the commandments of the Lord.

It is reported that on one occasion when Sir Isaac Newton was thinking seriously concerning the nature of light, he cut a hole in a window blind and a ray of light entered his room. He held a triangular piece of glass in the range of the light, and there were reflected in great beauty all the colors of the rainbow. And for the first time man learned that all of the glorious colors of the universe are locked up in a ray of white light.

It is important that we live all the principles of the gospel and obey all the commandments that the Lord has given us if we are to grow more nearly like our Father and his Beloved Son. We cannot say, "Oh, I believe in missionary work—it is important; I am thoroughly converted to the welfare plan or the wonderful social program of the Church for its young people; but I don't believe that Joseph Smith was a prophet or that our present prophets are guided by revelation from the Lord."

Some may say, "I believe the Book of Mormon, but I can't believe that it was received from an angel as Joseph said it was."

With a wavering faith of that kind, how can such a person expect to have the true light of Christ, the true understanding and light of the gospel? How can he expect to receive the blessings that the Lord has promised to the faithful? If he leaves out any one of these principles, he does not get pure white light. If he fails to have faith in all the principles of the gospel and does not have faith to live in accordance therewith, he cannot expect to get the pure light of the gospel in his heart.

If you truly have faith in God sufficient to impel you to keep his commandments, you will draw nearer to him and he will come nearer to you, and your faith will become knowledge, and the limit of your horizon will extend into the eternal world.

May we grow in faith through the love and blessing of our Lord and Savior, and may we keep the commandments that he has given us, that we may ultimately find salvation and exaltation in his celestial kingdom.

FASTING
AND PRAYER

Elder Robert L. Simpson

One of the most neglected and yet most needed laws for this troubled generation in a modern world of acceleration and distraction is the law of the fast. Fasting and praying have been referred to almost as a singular function from the earliest times. Adam's generation fasted and prayed, as did Moses on Sinai. (Deuteronomy 9:9-11.)

The prophet Elijah traveled to Mt. Horeb under the influence of fasting and prayer. There he received the word of the Lord. His preparation had not been in vain. (1 Kings 19:8.)

Mordecai's advice from Esther as he faced an emergency at Shushan pointed out that he and his people should "neither eat nor drink three days, night or day. . . ." (Esther 4:16.) This was the true fast, abstinence from both food and drink. This is still the manner of the true fast in our day.

There were significant changes made at the time of Christ's mission in mortality. The law of sacrifice, for example, was replaced by a higher law. We are told that following the Master's visit to this, the Western Hemisphere, the people were told to continue in "fasting and prayer [there was no change in this law] and in meeting together oft both to pray and to hear the word of the Lord." (4 Nephi 12.) So complete and sincere were the people in obeying his commandments "that there was no contention among all the people, in all the land; but there were mighty miracles wrought among the disciples of Jesus." (4 Nephi 13.) Wouldn't it be thrilling to enjoy such a condition today!

Christ's law has been reconfirmed in our day, for through a modern prophet in the year 1832, he said: ". . . I give unto you a commandment that ye shall continue in prayer and fasting from this time forth." Then he mentioned gospel teaching almost as a prime product of the prayer and fasting process. In the words of the Lord: "And I give unto you a commandment that you shall teach one another the doctrine of the kingdom. Teach ye diligently and my grace shall attend you, that you may be instructed more perfectly in theory, in principle, in doctrine, in the law of the gospel, in all things that pertain unto the kingdom of God, that are expedient for you to understand." (D&C 88:76-78.)

No man or woman can hope to teach of things spiritual unless he is directed by that spirit, for "the Spirit shall be given unto you by the prayer of faith; and if ye receive not the Spirit ye shall not teach.

"And all this ye shall observe to do as I have commanded concerning your teaching, until the fulness of my scriptures is given.

"And as ye shall lift up your voices by the Comforter, ye shall speak and prophesy as seemeth me good;

"For, behold, the Comforter knoweth all things, and beareth record of the Father and the Son." (D&C 42:14-17.)

Oh, that every teacher might catch the spirit of this promise and claim this offered partnership, available to all who are engaged in the teaching of all truth!

There are no better examples of teaching by the Spirit than the sons of Mosiah. The Book of Mormon tells us how they became "strong in the knowledge of the truth; for they were men of a sound understanding and they had searched the scriptures dilligently, that they might know the word of God.

"But this is not all; they had given themselves to much prayer, and fasting; therefore they had the spirit of prophecy, and the spirit of revelation, and when they taught, they taught with power and authority of God." (Alma 17:2-3.)

Is there a priesthood or auxiliary leader any place in this church who wouldn't give all to possess such power, such assurance? Remember this, above all else, that according to Alma, they gave themselves to much fasting and prayer. You see, there are certain blessings that can only be fulfilled as we conform to a particular law. The Lord made this very clear through the Prophet Joseph Smith when he declared: "For all who will have a blessing at my hands shall abide the law which was appointed for that blessing, and the conditions thereof, as were instituted from before the foundation of the world." (D&C 132:5.)

Now, the Lord could not have stated the position more clearly, and, in my opinion, too many Latter-day Saint parents today are depriving themselves and their children of one of the sweetest spiritual experiences that the Father has made available to them.

In addition to the occasional fasting experience for a special purpose, each member of the Church is expected to miss two meals on the fast and testimony Sunday. To skip two consecutive meals and partake of the third normally constitutes approximately a twenty-four-hour period. Such is the counsel.

Competent medical authorities tell us that our bodies benefit by an occasional fasting period. That is blessing number one and perhaps the least important. Second, we contribute the money saved from missing the meals as a fast offering to the bishop for the poor and the needy. And third, we reap a particular spiritual benefit that can come to us in no other way. It is a sanctification of the soul for us today just as it was for some choice people who lived two thousand years ago: "Nevertheless they did fast and pray oft, and did wax stronger and stronger in their humility, and firmer and firmer in the faith of Christ, unto the filling their souls with joy and consolation, yea, even to the purifying and the sanctification of their hearts, which sanctification cometh because of their yielding their hearts unto God." (Helaman 3:35.) Wouldn't you like this to happen to you? It can, you know!

Did you notice the scripture says that those who do this have their souls filled with "joy and consolation"? You see, the world in general thinks that fasting is a time for "sackcloth and ashes," a time to carry a look of sorrow, as one to be pitied. On the contrary, the Lord admonishes: "Moreoever when ye fast, be not, as the hypocrites, of a sad countenance: for they disfigure their faces, that they may appear unto men to fast. Verily I say unto you, They have their reward.

"But thou, when thou fastest, anoint thine head, and wash thy face;

"That thou appear not unto men to fast, but unto thy Father which is in secret: and thy Father, which seeth in secret, shall reward thee openly." (Matthew 6:16-18.)

Now, may we turn to the most important part of this great law. So far we have only discussed those areas that bless us. The real joy comes with the blessing of the poor and the needy. For it is in the fulfillment of this wonderful Christlike act that we practice "pure religion and undefiled" spoken of by James. Can you think of a better or more perfect Christian function than "pure religion and undefiled"? I can't.

The Lord speaking through Moses observed: "If there be among you a poor man of one of thy brethren within any of thy gates in thy land which the Lord thy God giveth thee, thou shalt not harden thy heart, nor shut thine hand from thy poor brother: But thou shalt open thine hand wide unto him. . . ." Then he goes on to promise him who gives: ". . . the Lord thy God shall bless thee in all thy works, and in all that thou puttest thine hand unto." He concludes: ". . . therefore I command thee, saying, Thou shalt open thine hand wide unto thy brother, to thy poor, and to thy needy, in thy land." (Deuteronomy 15:7-8, 10-11.)

Amulek had something to say on this subject. After instructing the people for some time on various vital matters, he turned his thoughts to the poor and the needy, advising the congregation that even if they are diligent in all of these other things, and "turn away the needy, and the naked, and visit not the sick and afflicted, and impart of your substance . . . to those who stand in need—I say unto you, if ye do not any of these things, behold, your prayer is vain, and availeth you nothing, and ye are as hypocrites who do deny the faith." (Alma 34:28.)

Yes, the law of the fast is a perfect law, and we cannot begin to approach perfection until we decide to make it a part of our lives. When you start and stop the fast is up to you, but wouldn't it be nice to culminate it and be at your spiritual peak for the fast and testimony meeting?

How much you give the bishop as a donation is also up to you, but isn't it thrilling to know that your accounting with the Lord has been paid willingly and with accuracy?

Why you fast is also up to you. But suppose the main reason was simply that you wanted to help someone in need and to be a part of "pure religion undefiled." Wouldn't your faith be lifted and sanctified? Of couse it would. And incidentally, have you ever noticed how satisfying it is way deep inside each time you are obedient to Heavenly Father's desires? There can be no equal to the peace of mind that always comes as the reward for obedience to truth.

The world needs self-discipline. It can be found in fasting and prayer. Our generation is sick for lack of self-control.

Fasting and prayer help to instill this virtue.

The world's future depends upon an urgent return to family unity. Fasting and prayer will help to guarantee it. Each person has greater need for divine guidance. There is no better way. We all have need to overcome the powers of the adversary. His influence is incompatible with fasting and prayer.

There can be no greater joy than in helping others, for "inasmuch as ye have done it unto one of the least of these my brethren, ye have done it unto me." (Matthew 25:40.)

And now, I join my testimony with Alma of old when he declared: ". . . Behold, I testify unto you that I do know that these things whereof I have spoken are true. And how do ye suppose that I know of their surety?

"Behold, I say unto you they are made known unto me by the Holy Spirit of God. Behold, I have fasted and prayed many days that I might know these things of myself. And now I do know of myself that they are true; for the Lord God hath made them manifest unto me by his Holy Spirit. . . ." (Alma 5:45-46.)

ADVERSITY
AND PRAYER

Bishop H. Burke Peterson

A young mother once said to me, "It seems in our home we go from one crisis to another. We never seem to be in calm waters. Either it's sick children, a Primary lesson to prepare, a car that breaks down before meetings, a flooded bathroom—you name it, we've had it." I suppose there are many whose life pattern would echo that refrain, even though the experiences will vary with each of us.

Because of the countless problems surrounding us and because of the trials and tribulations we are all confronted with, I've felt a need to be built up again in our understanding of why we have adversity and what we can do to weather its storm. It seems that life is filled with a variety of difficult experiences that test us and try us.

We should understand that a life filled with problems is no respecter of age or station in life. A life filled with trials is no respecter of position in the Church or social standing in the community. Challenges come to the young and to the aged, to the rich and to the poor, to the struggling student or the genius scientist, to the farmer, carpenter, lawyer, or doctor. Trials come to the strong and to the weak, to the sick and to the healthy. Yes, trials come even to the simplest child as well as to a prophet of God. At times they seem to be more than we can bear.

Now, some will say, "Why would a Father in heaven who calls us his children, who says he loves us above all of his creations, who says he wants only the best for us, who wants us to be happy and enjoy life to the fullest—why does he let these things happen to us, if we are really that dear to him?" The scriptures and the prophets have some needed answers for us.

We read in Helaman: "And thus we see that except the Lord doth chasten his people with many afflictions, yea, except he doth visit them with death and with terror, and with famine and with all manner of pestilence, they will not remember him." (Helaman 12:3.)

At a recent stake conference the stake president called a young father, who had just been ordained an elder, from the audience to bear his testimony. The father had been active in the Church as a boy, but during his teenage years he had veered somewhat from his childhood pattern. After returning from military service he married a lovely girl and presently children blessed their home. Without warning an undisclosed illness overcame their little four-year-old daughter. Within a very short time she was on the critical list in the hospital. In desperation and for the first time in many years the father went to his knees in prayer, asking that her life be spared. As her condition worsened and he sensed that she would not live, the tone of the father's prayers changed; he no longer asked that her life be spared, but rather for a blessing of understanding: "Let thy will be done," he said. Soon the child was in a coma, indicating her hours on earth were few. Now, fortified with understanding and trust, the young parents asked for one more favor of the Lord. Would he allow her to awaken once more that they might hold her closely? The little one's eyes opened, her frail arms stretched out to her mother and then to her daddy for a final embrace. When the father laid her on the pillow to sleep till another morning, he knew their prayers had been answered—a kind, understanding Father in heaven had filled their needs as he knew them to be. His will had been done—they were determined now to live so that they might live again with her.

Do you remember the words of the Lord to the Prophet Joseph Smith when he was having that great test of his faith in the Liberty Jail? The Lord said, "If thou art called to pass through tribulation . . ." and he enumerated a series of possibilities that would test any man to the utmost. He then concluded: "Know thou, my son, that all these things shall give thee experience and be for thy good." (D&C 122:5, 7.)

It's interesting to note that from the depths of trial and despair have come some of the most beautiful and classic passages of modern-day scripture—not from the ease of a comfortable circumstance. Might this also be the case in our own lives! From trial comes refined beauty.

We could cite Beethoven or Abraham Lincoln or Demosthenes who won out in a most difficult struggle to become a magnificent orator—but closer to us we see the great beauty and wisdom in the speaking and teaching of President Spencer W. Kimball and we see the price he's paid that our lives might be blessed.

In speaking of the Savior, the scriptures tell us: "Though he were a Son, yet learned he obedience by the things which he suffered." (Hebrews 5:8.)

From Hebrews we also read: "My son, despise not thou the chastening of the Lord, nor faint when thou art rebuked of him: for whom the Lord loveth he chasteneth, and scourgeth every son whom he receiveth." (Hebrews 12:5.)

Let us remember—trials are an evidence of a Father's love. They are given as a blessing to his children. They are given as opportunities for growth.

Now, how do we approach them? How do we overcome them? How are we magnified by them? There seems to be a reason why we lose our composure in adversity—why we think we can no longer cope with what we're faced with here in this life. There is a reason why we give up, why we "fall apart at the seams," so to speak. The reason may be so simple that we lose sight of it.

Could it be because we begin to lose contact with our greatest source of strength—our Father in heaven? He is the key to our enjoying sweetness in adversity—in gaining strength from our trials—he and he alone.

As a reassurance to us, let us read from the New Testament: "There hath no temptation taken you but such as is common to man: but God is faithful, who will not suffer you to be tempted above that ye are able; but will with the temptation also make a way to escape, that ye may be able to bear it." (1 Corinthians 10:13.)

Did you get the significance of that scriptural promise? We will have no temptation or trial beyond our ability to overcome. He will provide a way for us to rise above whatever the trial may be.

May I suggest that the best way I know to keep close to the source of this great strength is through prayer. No man can stand alone in his struggle through life. Sometimes in discouragement our prayers, at best, become occasional or maybe not at all. Sometimes we forget or just don't care.

Some may think that because they have a Word of Wisdom problem or because they have been dishonest or immoral, because they have not prayed for years, because of many reasons, they are now unworthy. "It's too late. I've made so many mistakes—so why even try?" To these we say, "For your own sake, give yourself another chance."

Sincere prayer is the heart of a happy and productive life. Prayer strengthens faith. Prayer is the preparation for miracles. Prayer opens the door to eternal happiness. The Father of us all is personal, ever waiting to hear from us, as any loving father would his children. To learn to communicate with him, to learn to pray effectively, requires diligence and dedication and desire on our part. I wonder sometimes if we are willing to pay the price for an answer from the Lord.

As we learn to develop this two-way communication, the standard of our life will improve. We will see things more clearly; we will try harder to do better; we will see the real joy that can come through trials and testing. Although problems will still be with us, peace, contentment, and true happiness will be ours in abundance.

As you feel the need to confide in the Lord or to improve the quality of your visits with him—to pray, if you please—may I suggest a process to follow: go where you can be alone, where you can think, where you can kneel, where you can speak out loud to him. The bedroom, the bathroom, or a closet will do. Now, picture him in your mind's eye. Think to whom you are speaking. Control your thoughts—don't let them wander. Address him as your Father and your friend. Now tell him things you really feel to tell him—not trite phrases that have little meaning, but have a sincere, heartfelt conversation with him. Confide in him. Ask him for forgiveness. Plead with him. Enjoy him. Thank him. Express your love to him. Then listen for his answers. Listening is an essential part of praying. Answers from the Lord come quietly, ever so quietly. In fact, few hear his answers audibly with their ears. We must be listening carefully or we will never recognize them. Most answers from the Lord are felt in our heart as a warm, comfortable expression, or they may come as thoughts to our mind. They come to those who are prepared and who are patient.

Yes, the trials will still be there; but with the companionship of the Spirit, our approach to trials will change frustrations and heartaches to blessings.

Just for a moment, think with me. Forget the trials you now have. Remember back to those trials you had last year, five years ago, ten years ago. What did you gain? What did you learn? Aren't you better prepared now because of them?

I testify the Lord is ready and waiting to help us. For our own good we must take the first step, and this step is prayer.

IMPROVING COMMUNICATION WITH OUR HEAVENLY FATHER

President Ezra Taft Benson

All through my life the counsel to depend on prayer has been prized above almost any other advice I have ever received. It has become an integral part of me, an anchor, a constant source of strength, and the basis of my knowledge of things divine.

"Remember that whatever you do or wherever you are, you are never alone," was my father's familiar counsel. "Our Heavenly Father is always near. You can reach out and receive his aid through prayer." I have found this counsel to be true. Thank God we can reach out and tap that unseen power, without which no man can do his best.

The holy scriptures are replete with convincing admonitions regarding the importance of prayer, impressive examples of prayer, and counsel on how to pray effectively.

During his earthly ministry Jesus said, ". . . men ought always to pray, and not to faint." (Luke 18:1.) "Watch and pray," he said, "that ye enter not into temptation." (Matthew 26:41.) In this dispensation he said, ". . . pray always lest that wicked one have power in you, and remove you out of your place." (D&C 93:49.)

Through Joseph Smith the warning came, "And in nothing doth man offend God, or against none is his wrath kindled, save those who confess not his hand in all things, and obey not his commandments." (D&C 59:21.)

Then we have this instruction from our risen Lord as he ministered among the Nephite people on this Western Hemisphere:

". . . ye must watch and pray always, lest ye be tempted by the devil, and ye are led away captive by him.

". . . ye must watch and pray always lest ye enter into temptation; for Satan desireth to have you, that he may sift you as wheat.

"Therefore ye must always pray unto the Father in my name;

"And whatsoever ye shall ask the Father in my name, which is right, believing that ye shall receive, behold it shall be given unto you." (3 Nephi 18:15, 18-21.)

May I now suggest some ways to improve our communication with our Heavenly Father.

1. *We should pray frequently.* We should be alone with our Heavenly Father at least two or three times each day: ". . . morning, mid-day, and evening," as the scripture indicates. (Alma 34:21.) In addition, we are told to pray always. (2 Nephi 32:9; D&C 88:126.) This means that our hearts should be full, drawn out in prayer unto our Heavenly Father continually. (Alma 34:27.)

2. *We should find an appropriate place where we can meditate and pray.* We are admonished that this should be "in your closets, and your secret places, and in your wilderness." (Alma 34:26.) That is, it should be free from distraction, in secret. (3 Nephi 13:5-6.)

3. *We should prepare ourselves for prayer.* If we don't feel like praying, then we should pray until we do feel like praying. We should be humble. (D&C 112:10.) We should pray for forgiveness and mercy. (Alma 34:17-18.) We must forgive anyone against whom we have bad feelings. (Mark 11:25.) Yet, the scriptures warn, our prayers will be vain if we "turn away the needy, and the naked, and visit not the sick and afflicted, and impart [not] of [our] substance. . . ." (Alma 34:28.)

4. *Our prayers should be meaningful and pertinent.* We should not use the same phrases at each prayer. Each of us would become disturbed if a friend said the same few words to us each day, treated the conversation as a chore, and could hardly wait to finish in order to turn on the TV and forget us.

In all of our prayers it is well to use the sacred pronouns of the scriptures—*thee, thou, thy,* and *thine* when addressing Deity in prayer, instead of the more common pronouns *you, your,* and *yours.* In this arrangement we show greater respect to Deity.

For what should we pray? We should pray about our work, against the power of our enemies and the devil, for our welfare and the welfare of those around us. (Alma 34:20; 22:25, 27.) We should counsel with the Lord pertaining to all our decisions and activities. (Alma 37:36-37.) We should be grateful enough to give thanks for all we have. (D&C 59:21.)

We should confess his hand in all things. Ingratitude is one of our great sins.

The Lord has declared in modern revelation: "And he who receiveth all things with thankfulness shall be made glorious; and the things of this earth shall be added unto him, even an hundred fold, yea, more." (D&C 78:19.)

We should ask for what we need, taking care that we not ask for things that would be to our detriment. (James 4:3.) We should ask for strength to overcome our problems. (Alma 31:31-33.) We should pray for the inspiration and well-being of the President of the Church, the General Authorities, our stake president, our bishop, our quorum president, our home teachers, our family members, and our civic leaders. Many other suggestions could be made, but with the help of the Holy Ghost, we will know about what we should pray. (Romans 8:26.)

5. *After making a request through prayer, we have a responsibility to assist in its being granted.* We should listen. Perhaps while we are on our knees, the Lord wants to counsel us. "Sincere praying implies that when we ask for any virtue or blessing, we should work for the blessing and cultivate the virtue." (David O. McKay.)

When I was a young missionary in northern England in 1922, opposition to the Church became very intense. The opposition became so strong that the mission president asked that we discontinue all street meetings, and in some places tracting was also discontinued.

My companion and I had been invited to travel over to South Shields and speak in sacrament meeting. In the invitation we were told, "We feel sure we can fill the little chapel. Many of the people over here do not believe the falsehoods printed about us. If you'll come, we're sure that we'll have a great meeting." We accepted.

We fasted and prayed sincerely and went to the sacrament meeting. My companion had planned to talk on the first principles of the gospel. I had studied hard in preparation for a talk on the apostasy. There was a wonderful spirit in the meeting. My companion spoke first and gave an inspirational message. I responded and talked with a freedom I had never experienced before in my life. When I sat down, I realized that I had not mentioned the apostasy. I had talked on the Prophet

Joseph Smith and borne my witness of his divine mission and to the truthfulness of the Book of Mormon. After the meeting ended, many people came forward, including several non-members, and said, "Tonight we received a witness that Mormonism is true. We are now ready for baptism."

This was an answer to our fasting and prayers, for we prayed to say only those things which would touch the hearts of the investigators.

In 1946 I was assigned by President George Albert Smith to go to wartorn Europe to reestablish our missions from Norway to South Africa, and to set up a program for the distribution of welfare supplies—food, clothing, bedding, etc.

We established headquarters in London. We then made preliminary arrangements with the military on the continent. One of the first men I wished to see was the commander of the American forces in Europe. He was stationed in Frankfurt, Germany.

When we arrived in Frankfurt, my companion and I went in to seek an appointment with the general. The appointment officer said, "Gentlemen, there will be no opportunity for you to see the general for at least three days. He's very busy and is filled up with appointments." I said, "It is very important that we see him and we can't wait that long. We're due in Berlin tomorrow." He said, "I'm sorry."

We left the building, went out to our car, removed our hats, and united in prayer. We then went back into the building and found a different officer at the appointment post. In less than fifteen minutes we were in the presence of the general. We had prayed that we would be able to see him and to touch his heart, knowing that all relief supplies contributed from any source were required to be placed into the hands of the military for distribution.

Our objective, as we explained it to the general, was to distribute our own supplies to our own people, through our own channels, and also make gifts for general child feeding. We explained the welfare program and how it operated. Finally, he said, "Well, gentlemen, you go ahead and collect your supplies, and by the time you get them collected, the policy may be changed." We said, "General, our supplies are already collected, they're always collected. Within twenty-four hours from the time I wire the First Presidency of the Church in Salt Lake City, carloads of supplies will be rolling toward Germany. We have many storehouses filled with basic commodities." He then said, "I've never heard of a people with such vision." His heart was touched as we had prayed it would be. Before we left his office we had a written authorization to make our own distribution to our own people through our own channels.

It is soul-satisfying to know that God is mindful of us and ready to respond when we place our trust in him and do that which is right. There is no place for fear among men and women who place their trust in the Almighty, who do not hesitate to humble themselves in seeking divine guidance through prayer. Though persecutions arise, though reverses come, in prayer we can find reassurance, for God will speak peace to the soul. That peace, that spirit of serenity, is life's greatest blessing.

As a boy in the Aaronic Priesthood, I learned this little poem about prayer. It has remained with me.

> *I know not by what methods rare,*
> *But this I know: God answers prayer.*
> *I know that He has given His word,*
> *Which tells me prayer is always heard,*
> *And will be answered soon or late,*
> *And so I pray and calmly wait.*
>
> *I know not if the message sought*
> *Will come just in the way I thought;*
> *But leave my prayers with Him alone*
> *Whose ways are wiser than my own,*
> *Assured that He will grant my quest,*
> *Or send some answer far more blessed.*

I bear witness that God lives. He is not dead. I bear testimony that God, our Father, with his Beloved Son, our Savior, did in very deed appear to Joseph Smith. I know this as I know that I live.

I testify that there is a God in heaven who hears and answers prayer. I know this to be true, for he has answered mine. I would humbly urge all persons—member and nonmember alike—to keep in close touch with our Father in heaven through prayer. Never before in this gospel dispensation has there been a greater need for prayer. That we will constantly depend upon our Heavenly Father and conscientiously strive to improve our communication with him is my earnest plea.

GREAT PERSONS WHO HAVE BELIEVED IN PRAYER

Elder John H. Vandenberg

"Prayer has always been a vital, personal force in my life." These are the words of one of America's great military heroes, James Doolittle. His life has been one of courage, a life guided by prayer. It is a sign of maturity when a person seeks the Lord's assistance in his day-to-day challenges. Many great persons have learned, as did Jimmy Doolittle, that their efforts are in vain unless they are assisted and directed by the Lord.

Benjamin Franklin, in urging the members of the Constitutional Convention to include prayer as part of its proceedings, said:

"I have lived, Sir, a long time; and the longer I live, the more convincing proofs I see of this truth; that God governs in the affairs of men. And, if a sparrow cannot fall to the ground without his notice, is it probable that an empire can rise without his aid? We have been assured, Sir, in the Sacred Writings, that 'except the Lord build the house, they labor in vain that build it.' I firmly believe this; and I also believe, that, without his concurring aid, we shall succeed in this political building no better than the builders of Babel; we shall be divided by our little, partial, local interests, our projects will be confounded, and we ourselves shall become a reproach and a by-word down to future ages. And, what is worse, mankind may hereafter, from this unfortunate instance, despair of establishing government by human wisdom, and leave it to chance, war, and conquest.

"I therefore beg leave to move, That henceforth prayers, imploring the assistance of Heaven, and its blessings on our deliberations, be held in this assembly every morning before we proceed to business; and that one or more of the clergy of this city be requested to officiate in that service." (Jared Sparks, *The Works of Benjamin Franklin*, 1837, pp. 155-56.)

Another of the delegates to that convention, Charles Pinckney, declared: "When the great work was done and published, I was . . . struck with amazement. Nothing less than that superintending hand of Providence, that so miraculously carried us through the war . . . , could have brought it about so complete, upon the whole." (L. L. Ford, ed., *Essays on the Constitution*, 1892, p. 412.)

James Madison, who became our fourth President and who had been sometimes called the "Father of the Constitution," wrote: "It is impossible for the man of pious reflection not to perceive in it a finger of that Almighty hand which has been so frequently and signally extended to our relief in the critical stages of the revolution." (*Federalist*, no. 37.)

George Washington, leader of the Colonial troops in the Revolutionary War and first President of the United States, acknowledged the hand of God on many occasions during the early struggles to establish independence and a new nation. In a letter to "the Executive of New Hampshire" on November 3, 1789, he wrote: "The success, which has hitherto attended our united efforts, we owe to the gracious interposition of Heaven; and to that interposition let us gratefully ascribe the praise of victory, and the blessings of peace."

One of the most famous paintings of the Father of Our Country depicts George Washington on his knees at Valley Forge, during the bleak winter of 1777, when the Colonial forces were almost defeated by the cold, shortages of food, clothing, and military supplies, and discouragement. Mason L. Weems, biographer of Washington, wrote:

"In the winter of '77, while Washington, with the American army lay encamped at Valley Forge, a certain good old Friend [Quaker], of the respectable family and name of Potts, if I mistake not, had occasion to pass through the woods near head-quarters. Treading his way along the venerable grove, suddenly he heard the sound of a human voice, which as he advanced increased on his ear, and at length became like the voice of one speaking much in earnest. As he approached the spot with a cautious step, whom should he behold, in a dark natural bower of ancient oaks, but the commander in chief of the American armies on his knees at prayer! Motionless with surprise, friend Potts continued on the place till the general, having ended his devotions, arose, and, with a countenance of angel serenity, retired to headquarters: friend Potts then went home, and on entering his parlour called out to his wife, 'Sarah, my dear! Sarah! All's well! all's well! George Washington will yet prevail!'

" 'What's the matter, Isaac?' replied she; 'thee seems moved.'

" 'Well, if I seemed moved, 'tis no more than what I am. I have this day seen what I never expected. Thee knows that I always thought the sword and the gospel utterly inconsistent; and that no man could be a soldier and a christian at the same time. But George Washington has this day convinced me of my mistake.'

"He then related what he had seen, and concluded with this prophetical remark—'If George Washington be not a man of God, I am greatly deceived—and still more shall I be deceived if God do not, through him, work out a great salvation for America." (*The Life of Washington*, pp. 181-82.)

Thomas Jefferson, in his second inaugural address, said: "I shall need the favor of that Being in whose hands we are, who led our fathers, as Israel of old, from their native land and planted them in a country flowing with all the necessaries and comforts of life; who has covered our national infancy with His wisdom and power, and to whose goodness I ask you to join in supplication with me that He will enlighten the minds of your servants, guide their councils, and prosper their measures that whatsoever they do shall result in good and shall secure to you the peace, friendship and approbation of all nations."

President Abraham Lincoln sought our Heavenly Father when he had difficulties and needed Divine guidance. Here is an example from his life:

"General Sickles has noticed that before the portentous battle of Gettysburg, upon the result of which, perhaps, the fate of the nation hung, President Lincoln was apparently free from the oppressive care which frequently weighed him down. After it was all past, the general asked Lincoln how that was. He said:

" 'Well, I will tell you how it was. In the pinch of your campaign up there, when everybody seemed panic-stricken and nobody could tell what was going to happen, oppressed by the gravity of our affairs, I went to my room one day and locked the door and got down on my knees before Almighty God and prayed to Him mightily for victory at Gettysburg. I told Him that this war was His, and our cause His cause, but we could not stand another Fredericksburg or Chancellorsville. Then and there I made a solemn vow to Almighty God that if He would stand by our boys at Gettysburg, I would stand by Him, and He did stand by you boys, and I will stand by Him. And after that, I don't know how it was, and I cannot explain it, soon a sweet comfort crept into my soul. The feeling came that God had taken the whole business into His own hands, and that things would go right at Gettysburg, and that is why I had no fears about you." (John Wesley Hill, *Abraham Lincoln—Man of God*, pp. 339-40.)

On another occasion President Lincoln said, "I have been driven many times to my knees by the overwhelming conviction that I had nowhere else to go. My own wisdom, and that of all about me, seemed insufficient for the day."

Henry Ward Beecher, nineteenth century clergyman, wrote: "Prayer is the key of the morning and the bolt of the night." In our own day, Dale Carnegie, noted educator and writer, has said, "Prayer gives us a sense of sharing our burdens, of not being alone. Few of us are so strong that we can bear our heaviest burdens, our most agonizing troubles, all by ourselves. Sometimes our worries are of so intimate a nature that we cannot discuss them even with our closest relatives or friends. Then prayer is the only answer."

Other great Americans have echoed similar testimonies of prayer. Eddie Rickenbacker said, "Prayer has been the greatest source of power in my life. I learned to pray at my mother's knee, and still never retire at night without uttering those same simple prayers. I pray about my business problems, my friends, family, country. Prayer has saved my life on more occasions that I can remember."

General Douglas MacArthur, who led the U.S. military forces in the Pacific theater of operations in World War II, is reported to have said that God "has so often guided me through the shadow of death and . . . nerved me in my hours of lonely vigil and deadly decisions."

United Nations Ambassador Henry Cabot Lodge, Jr., in a letter to the seventy-five members of the United Nations, appealed to them to open their meetings with prayer. "I do so," he said, "in the conviction that we cannot make the United Nations into a successful instrument of God's peace without

God's help—and that with his help we cannot fail. To this end I propose that we ask for that help."

Many governmental leaders today recognize the need for God's help in their deliberations. Prayer breakfasts are often held at the White House, the Pentagon, the U.S. Senate and House of Representatives, and among state and local governmental leaders. Senator Jennings Randolph of West Virginia, who attends the regular prayer breakfasts in the Senate, said, "At the end, when we join our hands in prayer, you can feel the grips tightening. You sense that we are going out strengthened." (*Reader's Digest*, May 1974, p. 167.)

"At this year's National Prayer Breakfast, held in late January, Senator John C. Stennis (D., Miss.) moved the audience by telling them how much his prayers and the prayers of others had meant in his recovery from wounds suffered when he was shot during a robbery a year ago. 'Short, silent prayers were my rallying point,' he said. 'The chief surgeon told me, "A higher hand entered your case." I know that he means what he said.' " (Ibid., p. 168.)

The influence of prayer in strengthening family ties and marriages has been beautifully expressed by Catherine Marshall, widow of Peter C. Marshall, chaplain of the U.S. Senate. In her book *A Man Called Peter* she writes:

"Though like every normal couple, Peter and I were sometimes in disagreement, we found that these differences could never become serious or bitter so long as we could pray together. So thoroughly did we learn this lesson that it was one of the chief bits of advice Peter always gave to couples whose marriages were almost bankrupt. 'If you will get down on your knees together,' he would tell them, 'your difficulties will soon be solved. You just can't pray together and stay mad at each other.'

"After our household grew in numbers, we discovered, too, that family prayers did not take the place of more intimate husband-and-wife prayers. Moreover, such prayers together were needed for our routine everyday lives, rather than just at the time when difficulties or disagreements arose. Peter always spoke of these prayers as 'lubricants for the machinery of life.'

"That was a supremely accurate description. Thus we tried to have a few quiet moments together in our bedroom before breakfast. On those mornings when we gave our day into God's hands and asked Him to bless it, we found that for each of us the whole day went more smoothly. There was a reassuring feeling of accomplishment at the end of it. When we omitted this brief prayer time together, things became snarled. We felt that we were battling uphill against terrific odds for meager accomplishment."

Cecil B. DeMille, the motion picture director and producer who made *The Ten Commandments,* said, "I could not live a day without [prayer]. It is the greatest power in the world."

With our great wealth, our medical advances, and our plentiful comforts, some may find themselves ignoring the continual need they have to pray to our Father in heaven. Many today seem to be echoing the statement of Job's contemporaries, ". . . what profit should we have if we pray unto him?" (Job 21:15.)

There is a great need for every person to realize the importance of prayer as he builds his life, for it is true that "except the Lord build the house, they labour in vain that build it." (Psalm 127:1.)

Prayer can be a vital force in lives, but we must learn how to make our prayers effective. As children, our prayers may have been mere repetition of phrases that we had learned. As we mature, it is well to view prayer with greater depth and with greater significance. As President David O. McKay so beautifully expressed it:

"I hope that some day you will have a longing, a longing that seems to wring your soul (in expressing that hope I have your interest at heart) that you will meet a wall that seems insurmountable, impregnable; but if duty lies beyond that wall, do not stand back and say, 'I cannot do it.' You may aspire to do it, but that is not sufficient. Do what James . . . says: Ask God for power, but add to that faith, an acknowledgment of your own ability to do what you are able to do.

"You can walk from where you stand, up to the wall. When you get there, and you have gone as far as you can, you will find in answer to your prayer that there is a hidden ladder by which you can scale it, or there is a door which you could not see from where you were first standing. God's hand is shown. In that hour you become responsive to the Infinite, and you realize what it means to be entitled to the guidance of the Holy Ghost; and he will guide you in these things.

"Wisdom comes through effort. All good things require effort. That which is worth having will cost part of your physical being, your intellectual power and your soul power. 'Ask, and it shall be given you; seek, and ye shall find; knock, and it shall be opened unto you.' But you have to ask, you have to knock, you have to seek." (*Treasures of Life*, pp. 303-4.)

THE POWER
OF PRAYER

President N. Eldon Tanner

I have great faith in prayer. I constantly pray that those who doubt might be helped to see and understand that God is our Father, that we are his spirit children, that he is really there and has said, "Ask, and it shall be given you; seek, and ye shall find; knock, and it shall be opened unto you: For every one that asketh receiveth; and he that seeketh findeth; and to him that knocketh it chall be opened." (Matthew 7:7-8.)

I often wonder if we really realize the power of prayer, if we appreciate what a great blessing it is to be able to call on our Father in heaven in humble prayer, knowing that he is interested in us and that he wants us to succeed.

As the late Elder Richard L. Evans so beautifully said: "Our Father in heaven is not an umpire who is trying to count us out. He is not a competitor who is trying to outsmart us. He is not a prosecutor who is trying to convict us. He is a loving Father who wants our happiness and eternal progress and who will help us all he can if we will but give him in our lives an opportunity to do so with obedience and humility, and faith and patience."

To pray effectively, and to feel that one can be heard and have his prayers answered, one must believe that he is praying to a God who can hear and answer, one who is interested in his children and their well-being. The first record we have of anyone praying to the Lord is that recorded by Moses in these words: "And Adam and Eve, his wife, called upon the name of the Lord, and they heard the voice of the Lord from the way toward the Garden of Eden, speaking unto them, and they saw him not; . . . And Adam and Eve, his wife, ceased not to call upon God. . . ." (Moses 5:4, 16.)

Great and influential men have always prayed for divine guidance. Even this great nation was founded on prayer. U.S. Senator Strom Thurmond of South Carolina reminded us of this when he said:

"The Mayflower Compact, written in November of 1620, begins with a prayer, 'In the name of God,' and goes on to state: 'We . . . having undertaken, for the glory of God, . . . do by these presents solemnly and mutually in the presence of God, and of one another, covenant and combine ourselves together into a civil body politic.'

"Thus our nation began founded on prayer. The kneeling figure of George Washington through that bitter winter in Valley Forge is a part of this country that should never be forgotten. . . .

"The Constitutional Convention in June of 1787 had been meeting for weeks without agreement, when Benjamin Franklin rose to his feet and addressed George Washington:

" 'Mr. President: The small progress we have made after four or five weeks close attention and continual reasonings with each other . . . is a melancholy proof of the imperfection of the human understanding. . . . We have gone back to ancient history for models of government that now no longer exist. And we have viewed modern states . . . but find none of their constitutions suitable to our circumstances. . . . How has it happened, Sir, that we have not, hitherto, once thought of humbly applying to the Father of Light to illuminate our understandings?

" 'In the beginning of the contest with Britain, when we were sensible of danger, we had daily prayers in this room for divine protection.

" 'Our prayers, Sir, were heard; and they were generously answered. . . .

" 'I, therefore, beg leave to move:—

" 'That henceforth, prayers imploring the assistance of Heaven and its blessings on our deliberations be held in this assembly every morning before we proceed to business. ("A Priceless Asset," *Spotlight*, May 1966.)

This was done, and now we enjoy the fruits of their labors in answer to prayer. Prayer has never been outmoded in this great country. Abraham Lincoln, who prayed to the Lord continually for guidance, said: "It is the duty of nations as well as of men to own their dependence upon the overruling power of God, to confess their sins and transgressions in humble sorrow . . . and to recognize the sublime truth that those nations only are blessed whose God is the Lord."

President Dwight D. Eisenhower, at the time of his inauguration, petitioned the Lord: "Give us, we pray, the power to discern clearly right from wrong, and to allow all our works and actions to be governed thereby, and by the laws of this land . . . so that all may work for the good of our beloved country, and for thy glory. Amen."

Samuel F. B. Morse, inventor of the telegraph, said that whenever he could not see his way clearly, he knelt down and prayed for light and understanding.

We have that sweet and simple prayer recorded by astronaut Gordon Cooper while orbiting the earth: "Father, thank you, especially for letting me fly this flight. Thank you for the privilege of being able to be in this position, to be up in this wondrous place, seeing all these many startling, wonderful things that you have created."

I join with Senator Thurmond in his appeal to our people "to pray more, to examine the religious heritage of our country, and to see the benefit of seeking God's blessings. Prayer is the only way in which the finite can communicate with the infinite; . . . in which the visible may be in touch with the invisible. You may easily see, if you but examine the history of our Nation, that prayer and communication with God is the very cornerstone of our society. If you allow it to be abandoned now, you will be casting away the greatest asset this Nation, or any other nation, has ever known."

All of the prophets, from Adam to our present prophet, have prayed unceasingly for guidance, and even the Savior prayed continually to God the Eternal Father. We read, regarding the Savior: "And it came to pass in those days, that he went out into a mountain to pray, and continued all night in prayer to God." (Luke 6:12.)

The Lord has admonished all of us to pray, and through the prophet James has given us this promise: "If any of you lack wisdom, let him ask of God, that giveth to all men liberally, and upbraideth not; and it shall be given him. But let him ask in faith, nothing wavering. For he that wavereth is like a wave of the sea driven with the wind and tossed." (James 1:5-6.)

This promise is given to every one of us—high and low, rich and poor. It is universal, unrestricted to you and to me and to our neighbors. He has told us that we must believe and have faith in God. We should know that the Lord stands ready to help his children if they will put themselves in tune through prayer and by keeping his commandments. In fact, the Lord has said: "I, the Lord, am bound when ye do what I say; but when ye do not what I say, ye have no promise." (D&C 82:10.)

We must be prepared to recognize that God is the Creator of the world, and that he, through his Son Jesus Christ and his prophets, has given us in simple language information regarding man's relationship to God, our pre-earth existence, the purpose of our mission here on earth, and the fact that our postmortal existence, or our life after death, is real, and that what we do here will condition us for the world to come.

We must not be misled by the doctrines of men. All the studies of science and philosophy will never answer the question: "What is man and why is he here?" But it is answered clearly and simply in the gospel of Jesus Christ, and we are instructed: "If any of you lack wisdom, let him ask of God."

Let us be prepared to do this and not be as those to whom the Savior referred, when he said: ". . . well did Esaias prophesy of you, saying, This people draweth nigh unto me with their mouth, and honoureth me with their lips; but their heart is far from me. But in vain they do worship me, teaching for doctrines the commandments of men." (Matthew 15:7-9.)

Yes, it is important, and the Lord emphasizes that we must humble ourselves and accept the teachings of Jesus Christ and keep his commandments if we would expect him to hear and answer our prayers. We should all be prepared to say truthfully, as Paul did, in speaking to the Romans, "For I am not ashamed of the gospel of Christ: for it is the power of God unto salvation to every one that believeth. . . ." (Romans 1:16.)

It is difficult to understand why some cannot believe, or find it very hard to believe that God can hear and answer our prayers, and yet they believe that astronauts can leave the earth and travel in outer space at thousands of miles per hour and still be directed from home base; that they can keep in touch with home base and receive instructions and be led in their activities and then be brought back to a safe landing here upon the earth.

How can we question God's ability to hear and answer our

prayers and direct us in all things if we will but keep in tune with him, and at the same time have no doubt that marvelous machines and men can be sent out from the earth to the moon and there be directed by mere man here upon the earth?

We are as astronauts, sent out by God to fill our missions here upon the earth. He wants us to succeed. He stands ready to answer our prayers and assures us a safe landing as we return if we will but keep in touch with him through prayer and do as we are bid.

As we pray, however, are we prepared to ask the Lord to bless us as we answer his call or acknowledge and serve him?

Are we prepared to ask the Lord to forgive us as we forgive one another?

We may well stop and analyze our own situation. Do we wait until we are in trouble and then run to the Lord? As we pray, do we give orders to the Lord by saying, "Bless this," and "Bless that," "Give us this," and "Give us that," "Do this," and "Do that"?

Or do we pray that we might be led to do that which is right, or be blessed with those things which are for our best good? We should always pray for the desire and strength and determination to do the will of our Heavenly Father, and always stand ready to do his bidding.

Men pray for different reasons. Many are driven to their knees out of fear, and then only do they pray. Others go to the Lord when in dire need of immediate direction for which they know of no other place to go. Nations are called by their governments in case of a national tragedy, drought, or plague, famine or war, to call upon God for his blessings, for his protection, and for his direction. Some people ask to be healed, others to be strengthened. They ask for the blessings of the Lord to attend their families, their loved ones, and themselves in all their righteous endeavors. This, I am sure, is all good in the sight of the Lord.

It is most important, however, that we take time to express our gratitude to our Father in heaven for the many blessings we receive.

As we express our appreciation for our many blessings, we become more conscious of what the Lord has done for us, and thereby we become more appreciative. We all know what it means to hear or receive an expression of gratitude for anything we might have done. Our forefathers set aside a day of thanksgiving. I fear that some of us even forget that day.

I wonder if we are sometimes guilty of not expressing to the Lord our gratitude, even as the lepers who were healed. We all remember so well the story of Jesus healing the ten lepers, who cried:

". . . have mercy on us.

"And one of them, when he saw that he was healed, turned back, and with a loud voice glorified God,

"And fell down on his face at his feet, giving him thanks: and he was a Samaritan.

"And Jesus answering said, Were there not ten cleansed? but where are the nine?

"There are not found that returned to give glory to God, save this stranger." (Luke 17:13, 15-18.)

And as Mark Antony said when referring to Caesar, who recognized his friend Brutus among his assassins:

This was the most unkindest cut of all;
For when the noble Caesar saw him stab,
Ingratitude, more strong than traitors' arms,
Quite vanquished him: then burst his mighty heart. . . .
—Julius Caesar, Act 3, sc. 2

I am sure that the Lord expects us to express our gratitude for our many blessings as we ask for his continued blessings, and to ask forgiveness for our failings and the desire and strength to do right.

When we pray, it is important that we set about to do all in our power to make it possible for the Lord to answer our prayers. As my father said to me when I was just a boy, "My son, if you want your prayers to be answered, you must get on your feet and do your part."

I often think how much more effective it would be, when the country's president calls upon his people to set aside a day of prayer, if we were all living righteous lives and were prepared to acknowledge God as our Creator and keep his commandments. It seems that many have lost belief in God entirely, and many question his ability to answer our prayers. Others have faith and confidence in their own learning and in their own strength and power.

The Lord has instructed parents to teach their children to

have faith in Christ, the Son of the living God, and to pray and to walk uprightly before the Lord. There is no doubt that our children, if they are taught to pray to a living God in whom they have faith, can more easily walk uprightly before the Lord.

I shall never be able to express fully my appreciation to my parents for teaching me to pray secretly and to participate with them in family prayer. My mother taught me at her knee. She made me feel and know that I was talking to the Lord, to our Maker, our Father in heaven, and that he was conscious of my acts and my wishes and my needs. I was taught that I should express my sincere thanks, ask for forgiveness, and ask for strength to do the right. This has always been a great strength to me throughout my life, and today I pray even more diligently than I ever did before that the Lord will guide and direct me in my activities, that whatever I do will be acceptable to him.

As I think back to when we used to kneel as a family in prayer every morning and every evening, I realize what it meant to us as children to hear our father call upon the Lord and actually talk to him, expressing his gratitude and asking for the blessings of the Lord on his crops and flocks and all of our undertakings. It always gave us greater strength to meet temptation when we remembered that we would be reporting to the Lord at night.

Family prayer in any home will draw the family closer together and result in better feelings between father and mother, between parents and children, and between one child and another. If children pray for their parents, it makes them more appreciative of their parents, and as they pray for one another, they feel closer to one another and part of each other, especially as they realize that they are talking to their Father in heaven while on their knees in family or secret prayer. Then is when we forget our differences and think of the best in others, and pray for their well-being and for strength to overcome our own weaknesses. There is no doubt that we are better people when we try to tune in to the spirit of our Father in heaven so that we might communicate with him and express our desire to do his will as we pray for his blessings.

The Lord has admonished us to "pray always, lest you enter into temptation and lose your reward. Be faithful unto the end, and lo, I am with you. These words are not of man nor of men, but of me, even Jesus Christ, your Redeemer, by the will of the Father." (D&C 31:12-13.)

I have often asked myself and tried to answer the question, Why do some people refuse to pray? Is it because they feel they have not the time?

I remember very well a father coming to me one day regarding his oldest son, with whom he was having some difficulty. The boy was a good boy, but he was getting out of hand. I asked the father if they had regular family prayers in their home. He answered, "Well, no, but sometimes. You know, we are too busy and we go to work at different times, and therefore it is most difficult for our family to get together for family prayer."

I asked, "If you knew that your boy was sick nigh unto death, would you be able to get your family together each night and morning for a week to pray that his life might be spared?"

"Why, of course," he said.

I tried then to explain to him that there are other ways of losing a boy than by death. I also explained that where families pray together, they usually stay together, and their ideals are higher, they feel more secure, and they have a greater love for one another.

Do people not pray because they feel too independent, too smart, and think they can go it alone? Or are they ashamed to call upon God? Do they think it shows a weakness? Or do they not believe in or have faith in God? Or is it that they do not appreciate their many blessings? Or do they not feel worthy? If one does not feel worthy, he should acknowledge his weaknesses, express regret, repent, covenant to do right, and ask for guidance.

Is it because some do not know how to pray? If that is true, I suggest that you go to your Heavenly Father in secret. Pour out your heart to him. Pray regularly so that you can feel at home and comfortable while communicating with him. All one needs to do is express his feelings, which the Lord understands. He has invited all of us to call on him regularly and has promised that he will hear our supplication.

The ancient prophet Moroni, referring to the Book of Mormon, said:

"And when ye shall receive these things, I would exhort you that ye would ask God, the Eternal Father, in the name of Christ, if these things are not true; and if ye shall ask with a sincere heart, with real intent, having faith in Christ, he will manifest the truth of it unto you, by the power of the Holy Ghost.

"And by the power of the Holy Ghost ye may know the truth of all things." (Moroni 10:4-5.)

This promise applies to all of us if we will but repent and go to the Lord, knowing that he can hear and will hear and answer our prayers. We should all realize that we are God's children and that he is still as interested in us as he ever was. He still answers the prayers of the righteous and those who diligently seek him.

THE LORD'S PRAYER

Elder S. Dilworth Young

I ask myself if I should pray,
And if I do, to whom?
The answer comes, just say:
Our Father which art in heaven.

And if I pray, what then?
How do I speak my love
And show profound respect?
Hallowed be thy name.

What should I ask of such
A Being as he who dwells
On high?
Thy kingdom come.

How do I conquer pride
Of heart and hand?
Thy will be done in earth,
As it is in heaven.

And do I ask for earthly
Things, the things of heart and head?
Give us this day our
Daily bread.

What if unworthiness be
Part and parcel of my heart?
And forgive us our debts,
As we forgive our debtors.

Where do I obtain the strength
To stand until the end?
And lead us not into temptation.

(More likely it will be that I
shall have to ask:
Leave me not in temptation.

The Lord won't lead me there.
I pray when I am there
I'll not be left without
His help.)

Those times when evil
Encompasses me about,
What do I say to him who
Dwells on high?
Deliver us from evil.

One praying from his heart
Will have the great desire to
Give all praise for each
Sustaining gift from God,
And so we end our prayer:
For thine is the kingdom,
And the power,
And the glory, forever.
Amen.

THOUGHTS
ON ALMA 34:17-29

Elder S. Dilworth Young

When Amulek was called to speak,
His sermon was not of the task today
But rather, one should pour
His soul out to the Lord,
And pray.
He named the items one
By one, including flocks
And herds
And home,
And further said that
When thus not engaged,
A loyal saint would
Carry in his heart and
Mind
A constant prayer for all of
Humankind.
And, having spoken to the Lord
These sacred private thoughts,
He then would
Share his goods with those
Who stood in need,
And turn not one away,
The poor, the sick, the weak,
Each day.

Prayers are answered quickly
When
One shows his love of God
By loving men.

OUR DEPENDENCE ON PRAYER

Elder S. Dilworth Young

I acknowledge my weakness when I pray,
My dependence on my God.
I hear him say:
Watch and pray, lest ye enter
Into temptation.[1]
He gives me power thus
To go my way
In truth, in righteousness
Each day,
Toward my redemption.

A little child being taught
To kneel and lisp a prayer
Learns as a babe to know
The Father's loving care.
And doubting not the faith that
Answer brings,
Goes through his life confirming
Heavenly things.

The youth who thus has early learned
To kneel and speak
To God,
To center hope and thought
On Him who gave him life,
Will rise up strong and true
In heavenly things,
His heart and soul take wings.

The maid who places faith
In God enough to pray
To him each day
Will find her soul filled

---

[1] Matthew 26:41.

As with a fire, an
All-consuming faith
Of heavenly desire.

The man who in his strength
Will humbly bow
His knee to plead for
Length of life and favor
Of the Lord,
Protecting care from
Tempters and those
Evil ones who seek
To break his promised
Word,
Will find that strength
To be a son of God
The Lord.

The wife who waits at home
At dusk
Her man's return
To comfort of her arms
May pray,
And praying,
Knows that he will
Come with strengthened
Soul, knowing she
Prayed for him
That day.

INDEX

Abinadi calls people to
repentance, 59-60
Adam: was commanded to pray,
16; ceased not to call upon
God, 123
Adversity, purpose for, 21, 105.
See also Crisis; Trials
Agency, prayer does not replace,
13, 21, 47-48, 50, 128. *See also*
Works
Air Force test flights, story of, 85
Airplane, story of praying on, in
storm, 76-77
Alma: was brought to repentance,
18; teaches poor about faith, 97
Amen, significance of saying, 14,
37-38
Amulek: lists what to pray for, 11,
17-18, 35; counsels people to
remember the needy, 15, 103
Answers to prayer: 18-19; God can
give, 1; come through Christ,
10; as stupor of thought or
burning, 25, 55; of
missionaries, 82; poem about,
114; come through work, 128
Apostles, choosing of early, 6-7
Ask, and ye shall receive, 9, 19, 68,
122, 123
Astronauts, analogy of, 126-27
Atonement: 5-6; set prayers relate
to, 56; necessary to exaltation,
56, 58, 63. *See also* Christ

Baptism: reason for, 60; symbolism
of, 60-61; set prayer for, 60, 61;
requirements for, 61-62;
accomplishments of, 62
Beecher, Henry Ward, quotation
concerning prayer, 119

Benedictions: length of, 40;
purpose of, 40
Birth, story of complications
accompanying, 89-90
Blessings: follow prayer, 9, 21, 71,
94; ask for temporal and
spiritual, 9, 10-11, 34-35, 112;
follow obedience, 101; trials
given as, 107
Brother of Jared was chastened for
not praying, 17

Carnegie, Dale, quotation
concerning prayer, 119
Chastening of the Lord, despise
not, 107
Children: must be taught to pray,
2, 85, 94; should offer family
prayer, 3; tongues of, loosed,
30; have special spirit of prayer,
30, 74, 89, 91, 94; learn by
example to pray, 30; are taught
to pray by goodly parents, 19,
75, 89; gain strength through
family prayer, 129; story of
orphan boy praying before
operation, 74-75
Christ: praying in Gethsemane,
5-7, 35; praying on the
mountain, 7, 125; praying for
his disciples, 47; birth of, 58-59;
praying for his Nephite
followers, 77-79
Commandment to pray, 9, 11, 16,
19
Communication with God: is
most vital of all, 4; prayer
allows, 8, 23-24, 129; leads to
knowledge of Him, 9; live
worthy of, 83, 130; learning,

Neal A. Maxwell

Marion D. Hanks

Joseph Anderson

John N. Vandenberg

Robert L. Simpson

S. Dilworth Young

Hartman Rector, Jr.

Carlos E. Asay

Vaughn J. Featherstone

J. Parker Peterson